The perfect PUMPKIN
and other
SQUASH

VALWYN McMONIGAL

PHOTOGRAPHY BY QUENTIN BACON
STYLING BY DONNA HAY

BayBooks

An imprint of HarperCollins*Publishers*

STOCKISTS

Corso De Fiori
355 South Dowling Street
Darlinghurst NSW 2010
Tel: (02) 360 5151

Appley Hoare Antiques
55 Queen Street
Woollahra NSW 2025
Tel: (02) 362 3045

A BAY BOOKS PUBLICATION

Bay Books, an imprint of
HarperCollinsPublishers
25 Ryde Road Pymble, Sydney NSW 2073, Australia
31 View Road, Glenfield, Auckland 10, New Zealand

First published in Australia in 1994

National Library of Australia
Cataloguing-in-Publication data:

  McMonigal, Valwyn.
    The perfect pumpkin and other squash.
    Includes index.
    ISBN 1 86378 182 X.

    1. Cookery (pumpkin). 2. Cookery (Squash). I. Title.

  641.6562

Front cover photography: Jon Bader
Internal photography: Quentin Bacon
Food stylist: Donna Hay
Food stylist's assistants: Jody Vassallo and Darienne Sutton
Assistant recipe testers: Deborah Hughes and Anne-Maree Kinley
Front cover recipes: Pumpkins with Chilli Beans, Pumpkins with Vegetable Stir-fry and Pumpkins
with Chicken and Coriander
Information on cultivation from Michael and Jude Fanton, Seed Savers' Handbook, Seed Savers'
Network, Byron Bay

Printed in Australia by Griffin Press, Adelaide

5 4 3 2 1
97 96 95 94

CONTENTS

The Perfect Pumpkin

The mouth watering aroma of freshly baked pumpkin scones, the smooth flavour of a golden soup or perhaps a slice of delicious pie can only begin to testify to the wonderful range of dishes the pumpkin can provide. To taste tiny pumpkins, crammed full of tempting fillings and baked to perfection, the wonderful richness of pumpkin ice-cream, or pumpkin simply cooked in its skin, with butter and freshly ground pepper, surely lifts the pumpkin from its humble beginnings to being one of the most versatile vegetables available. If you haven't indulged in cooking pumpkin cakes or puddings you are in for a sweet surprise, and for those who have scorned it as a savoury ingredient, try a pasta sauce or one of the tempting entrées, and pumpkin will be on your menu forever.

As with many vegetables, pumpkins and squashes can be added to soups and casseroles, and merely become a part of that dish, but they do have an individuality and the recipes that follow are created to bring forth that individuality. They illustrate the variety of uses that make the pumpkin and squash such versatile and interesting vegetables.

The pumpkin belongs to the Cucurbits family (known also as the Squash family) which is characterised mainly by vining varities. The plant is an annual. Occasionally, bushy varieties are grown. Included in this plant group are gourds, marrows, and melons (water, rock and oriental), as well as cucumbers, chokos, pumpkin and squashes.

In this cookbook, however, I have concentrated mainly on pumpkins (known as hard skinned squash in America), zucchini (courgettes) and added a little on chokos, cucumbers, and marrows. The common names for these vary from country to country and even region to region.

PUMPKIN

Cucurbita (gourd) maxima (largest)
The history of the pumpkin is most interesting as it is one of the oldest known vegetables, dating back to approximately 3000 BC, when it was first called pompions or pumpions from the Indian word pompom (round) and the Greek word, pepon (weighty).

The large, hard skinned vegetable originated in the Andean valleys and remained isolated there until the Spanish arrived and introduced the pumpkin to Central and Northern America. The pumpkin arrived in Europe in the 16th century, although it didn't flourish there as well as it did in warmer climates, and was used mainly for livestock fodder.

The pumpkin has a multitude of uses from deep frying the flower through to soups, breads and desserts. The uses for the pumpkin flesh are endless. When only the shell is left, that too can be used, as a table centre piece or a Jack O' Lantern for Hallowe'en. Oh! and don't forget to roast the seeds, they're delicious to nibble, as well as containing iron and protein.

Pumpkins have large prickly leaves, and like all other squashes, produce both male and female flowers. Only the male flowers have pollen which the bees transfer to the female flowers that are open for one day only. The pollinated female flowers then produce pumpkins. However, as most flowers are male, few flowers actually produce fruits. The male and female flowers are easily identified as within four days of flowering, the female flower has a bowl shaped end while the male flower remains thinner and straighter.

SQUASH AND MARROW
Cucurbita (gourd) pepo (pumpkin)
A nutritious vegetable, with at least forty varieties, featuring a multiple of shapes, sizes, colours and tastes.

Squash is a native of South America. The name, askutasquash, comes from a native Indian word meaning "eaten raw", and refers to the entire plant and fruit. The plant was developed in England as a garden vegetable in the 19th century. It was a great feature at country fairs, as many a farmer or garden enthusiast spent much time in cultivating the largest plant to take away the first prize.

ITALIAN MARROW OR ZUCCHINI (COURGETTE)
Cucurbita pepo
A close relative of the baby, or immature squash. Believed to have originated in Italy in the Po Valley some 300 years ago, but virtually unknown to the rest of the world until about 1950, where their simple growing habits and their availability throughout most of the year has made them a very popular vegetable. The name courgette is a derivative of the word sweetness. There are several different varieties in skin colour, from yellow through to deep green. They have a high water content and can be eaten with the skin on either raw or cooked. The flower is also an edible delicacy.

CHOKO
Sechium edule (edible)
Originally from Mexico and known there as chayote and as christophine in the West Indies. The Aztecs were eating them long before the Spanish arrived. The choko has travelled the world and can often be found hanging over a shed or back fence. There are many kinds of chokos, from smooth-skinned to prickly-skinned.

CUCUMBER
Cucumis sativus (cultivated)
Originally from northern India, the cucumber travelled to China in the 2nd century BC, and then to the Middle East. It is recorded in the Bible that the Israelites complained to Moses about the lack of cucumbers in the wilderness! The Romans cultivated them, and it is said that Charlemagne grew them in his 9th century garden. However, the Britons had to wait until the 14th century for their first cucumber salad. Columbus took the seeds of the cucumber with him to the Americas.

GOURDS
Lagenaria siceraria
Is the name given to a group of ornamental climbing or trailing plants, related to the pumpkin/ squash family. Grown wild in America, Asia, Pacific Islands and Africa, in various shapes and colours. It is estimated that the seeds of the African gourd floated to South America in approximately 5000 BC. In South America, the Indians carved intricate designs on the skins of the dried gourds and used them as ornaments or for carrying water. The dishcloth gourd is also known as luffa or loofah and is used as a bath sponge.

NUTRITIONAL VALUE
The nutritional value of a 160 g (5½ oz) serve of pumpkin is very good. It has a high vitamin A content (over 70%), levels of vitamin C and fibre are also good (over 50%) and its energy level is 282 kj (67 cal).

The nutritional value of a 150 g (4½ oz) serve of squash or zucchini (courgette) is also high. Its vitamin C level is good (over 70%). There is less vitamin A (less than 10%), fibre (less than 2%) and an energy level of 84 kj (20 cal).

VARIETIES OF PUMPKINS

Many strains of the pumpkin are grown. A few of the most popular, commercial varieties are listed below.

Baby Blue with fruit up to one metre in length. It has a soft, blue-grey skin and is very tasty.

Banana is a large, cylindrical vegetable with a soft blue-grey skin.

Big Blue Max is a large pumpkin with a thick skin, blue-grey in colour, round, with bright orange flesh.

Butterbush is similar to the Golden Nugget.

Butternut is a member of the Gramma family. An excellent vegetable, it is the most versatile of the pumpkins, being suitable for soups, desserts, scones and bread.

Cattle is a large, thin skinned variety and, as the name suggests, is used mainly for pig food.

Crown Prince is a drum shape, with a thin creamy-grey skin and rich-red flesh.

Green Warted Hubbard is a large fruit. It is tasty, with a tough skin.

Golden Delicious is a fast maturing and very tasty pumpkin but it doesn't keep well.

Golden Nugget is roughly the size of a grapefruit, keeps well and is sweet to taste. Ideal for stuffing.

Henderson Late Grey is large and will keep for quite a long time.

Jap has a thin, green skin with yellow patches. Its sweet, nutty flavour is enhanced by the use of herbs. Ideal for cakes, pies and soups.

Jarrahdale also keeps well. It has

a round, hard ribbed, slate-blue skin and is tasty, with bright orange flesh. Most suitable for cakes and desserts.

Queensland Blue is medium sized, round with a hard, deeply ribbed, slate grey skin. The 'Blue' is most suited for baking, and is perhaps the most popular variety.

Queensland Grey is slightly softer, but equally suitable for baking.

Red Hubbard is a large pumpkin with firm flesh.

Trombone is long and curved like a horse's collar, golden brown with sweet yellow flesh.

Triamble is also a large variety. It is tasty and keeps well.

Trippletreat keeps well and has hull-less seeds.

Windsor Black matures early, and has a dark green, multi-ribbed skin.

VARIETIES OF SQUASH

Squash is divided into two major groups: summer and winter.

Summer Squash grows mainly on bushes. The immature fruit is picked whilst the skin is still soft. If the summer squash is allowed to ripen, it becomes large and loses some of its flavour. Varieties of summer squash are listed below.

Cocozelle is a stripe-skinned zucchini.

Golzini and Gold Rush are hybrids, both are golden yellow.

Greyzini hybrid has a pale green skin.

President hybrid and Black Jack hybrid are very popular, with dark green skins.

Ronde de Nice are round, eaten in a ratatouille and are harvested when roughly the size of a cricket ball.

Round have a flattened top and bottom. Varieties include Old English, Tender and True.

Scallop is scallop-shaped and varieties include yellow bush, pattypan, white scallop, yellow and green button squash.

Yellow Crookneck is a curved, decorative plant.

Zucchini (courgette) are really immature marrows and are cylindrical with shiny green or golden skin. They can be eaten raw or cooked.

Winter Squash grow on vines and are picked fully ripe when the skin is hard.

Banana squash is often used in the preparation of baby foods.

Hubbard, another popular squash, is large and rough-skinned.

Vegetable Spaghetti is a yellow marrow-like fruit which can be forked out like spaghetti and is a great substitute for pasta. High in Vitamins A and C, folate and panthothen acid but low in calories.

VARIETIES OF CUCUMBERS

The most popular cucumbers are listed below.

Dill is used for pickling.

Telegraph or Contintental are an elongated, dark-skinned variety.

Apple Round have a tough skin which should always be removed.

Gherkin are small immature fruits, pickled and served as a savoury.

Lebanese is elongated, thin, pale skin, very crisp and ideal for salads.

African Horned is also known as bitter or jelly cucumber in Africa or kiwano in New Zealand, where it is eaten fully ripe, as a fruit.

BUYING AND STORING

Pumpkin is available fresh throughout the year and can be purchased whole or in pieces. Pick whole pumpkins when fully mature, leaving stalk on. Do not damage stalk, as rot will set in at the junction of stalk and fruit. If the stalk has been damaged or removed, drip wax from a candle onto the broken area of the stalk until it is completely sealed.

Look for firm skin and bright flesh. Store whole pumpkins in an airy, cool place or store pieces in refrigerator, removing seeds and membrane. They store well, uncooked, for at least one week.

Squash, choko, and cucumbers are available most of the year. Choose shiny firm-skinned fruit. Do not wash any fruit or vegetable until ready to use. Store in refrigerator or cool place.

COOKING AND PREPARATION TECHNIQUES

Pumpkin

Remove seeds, membrane and skin (or pumpkin can be boiled or baked in the skin, remove after cooking).

BOILING: Place chunky pieces or slices in a saucepan and cover with water, bring to the boil and boil gently until tender. Mash with butter or serve whole.

BAKING: Place pumpkin on a wire rack in a baking dish and cook at moderate temperature for approximately 40 minutes.

OVEN STEAMING: Place pieces on a wire rack over a pan of hot water in a moderate oven for approximately 40 minutes.

PRESSURE COOKING: A great way to retain colour and nutrients. It reduces the boiling time to about one-third of the normal time.

MICROWAVING: Peel, place pieces in microwave oven and cook on HIGH for approximately 6 minutes.

Whole Butternut: Pierce skin twice, place in a microwave and cook on HIGH for 20 minutes, stand for 5 minutes.

Whole Golden Nugget: Prick skin once, microwave on HIGH for 5 to 10 minutes (depending on size), stand 4 minutes.

STEAMING: Place a small amount of water in pan, bring to the boil, arrange slices in a steamer and place over boiling water. Steam until tender.

SEEDS: Allow seeds to dry, remove husk to reveal green skinned ivory-coloured flesh. These can be eaten raw or roasted in a slow oven until lightly brown. Can be bought in most health food shops.

MASHING: Boil, steam or microwave. Remove flesh from skin and mash with a little butter.

STEWING OR CASSEROLING: Cut into small pieces, place in covered dish with other vegetables and meat. Cook in oven or on top of hot plate for about one hour.

FREEZING: Peel and cook until tender, mash and spoon cool pulp into a container. Will freeze up to 6 months.

Squash

Summer squash are usually eaten with their skins on. Winter squash are usually cooked in the skin, then the flesh is removed for eating.

BOILING: Place in a pan with water just covering the squash. Bring to boil, simmer until tender, drain and serve.

BAKING: Not suitable.

STEAMING: Place whole or sliced in a steamer over a small quantity of boiling water. Steam until tender.

MICROWAVING: Whole or sliced. Place in a dish with 1 tablespoon of water. Cover and cook on HIGH for 3 minutes (depending on thickness of squash). Stand for 3 minutes.

MASHING: Either steam, microwave or boil, remove skins from winter squash, mash with a little butter.

STEWING OR CASSEROLING: Slice or dice. Add to other ingredients 20 minutes before cooking time elapses.

FREEZING: Not suitable.

NOTE: Steaming or boiling vegetables produces a soft texture, while microwaving retains a firmer texture.

Chokos

Chokos are usually peeled before cooking, unless very young and boiled, steamed or microwaved (on HIGH, for approximately 4 to 5 minutes each), until just tender, when they can be mashed, served whole with butter, or served with a white sauce.

Cucumbers

Cucumbers are usually served as a salad vegetable or pickled. If cooked they have a somewhat bitter taste.

HOME GROWING

There is nothing more enjoyable when preparing meals, than to gather vegetables straight from the garden, whilst the dew is sparkling on the plants. The flavour of freshly picked produce is far superior to any bought from the shops. Here are a few hints to help you produce a fine eating crop.

Pumpkin is best sown in spring, with the seeds planted directly into a compost heap and allowed to grow over a fence or shed. Small bush types such as Golden Nugget are ideal for small gardens. Fertiliser or mulch should be applied when flowers appear and repeated every three to four weeks while the plants are cropping. It is best to allow the pumpkins to stay on the vine until the vine dies down then pick, leaving a section of stalk still attached. It usually takes between 14 to 20 weeks from sowing to picking.

Squash (zucchini (courgette) and marrow) is also sown in spring, in temperate areas, whilst in tropical zones, seeds can be planted winter through to autumn. Plant in raised mounds, with three to four seeds per mound leaving a gap of 75 cm (30 in) between plants. Water only when soil is dry or when the fruits begin to swell, fertilise every fourteen days.

Zucchini (courgette) are picked whilst still small, and all squashes can be picked with the flower still attached. They take from 8 to 14 weeks from sowing to harvesting.

Cucumber can be sown in temperate areas from spring to summer. Seeds should be sown in compost mounds raised from surrounding soil. Once the seedlings shoot they should be thinned out to approximately 40 cm (16 in) between plants however, this does vary according to variety. Cucumbers need to be watered regularly although avoid wetting the leaves. They require a dressing of a complete plant food once flowering commences then every 4 to 5 weeks. For easy harvest, cucumbers can be trained to grow over a trellis. Cucumbers are ready for harvest 8 to 12 weeks after sowing.

Choko is a perennial vine that is extremely easy to grow in warm areas but sensitive to frost. It is a low maintenance crop and is grown from a sprouted fruit. The fruit should be planted with the sprout just showing above the ground and close to its support. Grow in well drained soil rich in organic matter. In winter, the vine dies down and should be cut back to approximately 15 cm (6 in) above ground. Chokos can be picked 18 to 24 weeks after sowing, when fully developed but still with a tender skin. Chokos grow best when allowed to hang over a fence or shed.

Soups and Starters

S oup is as old as the use of fire for cooking, when greens, roots and pieces of meat were thrown into a pot and simmered over an open fire, usually providing the only substantial meal of the day. This chapter takes a fresh look at a tired old stand by — Pumpkin Soup. We also show you wonderful starters and finger food, all using pumpkin and other squash.

PUMPKIN SOUP

500 g (1 lb) pumpkin

20 g (½ oz) butter

1 medium onion, sliced

1 medium potato, peeled and sliced

3 cups (750 ml/24 fl oz) chicken stock

choice of sour cream, nutmeg, parsley or herb of your choice, pastry shapes (see soup accompaniments page 19), to garnish.

Cut pumpkin into 8 wedges, peel, remove membrane. In a deep pan, melt butter and gently fry onion until transparent, add pumpkin, potato and stock. Cover and bring to the boil. Simmer for 40 minutes. Cool slightly, blend or push through strainer until smooth.

To Serve: Reheat, ladle into bowls, top with a swirl of sour cream, sprinkle with nutmeg or chopped herbs or parsley and float a pastry shape on top.

Suitable to freeze (without cream or garnishes).

Variation: Green Apple Soup
You will need 3 green skinned apples, peeled, cored and sliced.

Place the apple in the pan with the pumpkin and cook as with other ingredients. Proceed with the recipe as usual.

Serve with 2 thin unpeeled slices of apple floating in the soup and a sprinkling of grated tasty cheese.

SERVES 6

Pictured on previous pages: Zucchini (Courgette) and Tomato Soup (page 15), Poached Scallops with Pumpkin Purée (page 25), Cucumber Soup (page 15)

Pumpkin Soup (recipe above), Soufflé Oysters (page 26), Almond Crusted Balls (page 22)

MICROWAVE PUMPKIN SOUP

500 g (1 lb) butternut pumpkin

30 g (1 oz) butter

2 shallots or 1 medium onion, sliced

3 cups (750 ml/24 fl oz) chicken stock

½ cup (125 ml/4 fl oz) milk

24 croutons, ground nutmeg to garnish

Pierce skin of pumpkin several times. Place in centre of microwave turntable and cook on HIGH for 10 minutes. Cool. Place butter and onion in a deep container, microwave on HIGH for 2 minutes. Add half the chicken stock.

Cut pumpkin, remove membrane, scoop out flesh add to onion and stock mixture. Blend or push through a sieve until smooth. Return to deep container. Add remaining stock. Cover with lid or plastic wrap and microwave on HIGH for 5 minutes. Stir in milk. Reheat, on HIGH for 30 seconds.

To Serve: Ladle into bowls, float 4 croutons (see soup accompaniments page 19) on top, dust with nutmeg.

Variations: Add a sprig of fresh rosemary, blend with soup, or substitute dried rosemary for nutmeg.

Suitable to freeze (without garnishes).

SERVES 6

CONFETTI OF VEGETABLES

20 g (½ oz) butter

2 onions, peeled and finely diced

125 g (4 oz) zucchini (courgettes) ends removed, finely diced

1 red capsicum, (pepper), seeds removed, finely diced

1 green capsicum (pepper), seeds removed, finely diced

1 large potato, peeled and diced

2 sticks celery, diced

125 g (4 oz) can sweet corn kernels, drained

3 cups (750 ml/24 fl oz) water

1 vegetable stock cube

1 bay leaf

1 teaspoon dried thyme

freshly ground black pepper

2 rashers bacon, finely shredded and fried until crisp and drained, to garnish

Melt butter, gently fry onions until transparent. Add all ingredients, except bacon. Cover, bring to boil and simmer for 40 minutes. Remove bay leaf.

To serve: Sprinkle with crisp bacon shreds.

Suitable to freeze (without garnishes).

SERVES 6

PINDA BRAVOE

A hearty soup from Guyana.

500 g (1 lb) stewing beef, diced

5 cups (1.25 litres/40 fl oz) water

4 beef stock cubes

1 medium onion, diced

125 g (4 oz) pumpkin, peeled, membrane removed and diced

265 g (8½ oz) peanut butter

1 green capsicum (pepper), seeded and cut into thin strips

corn chips, to garnish

sour cream, to garnish

Place beef, water, stock cubes, onion and pumpkin into a deep pan. Cover and bring to the boil. Simmer for 2 hours. Place peanut butter in a bowl. Stir in 1 cup (250 ml/8 fl oz) beef stock until peanut butter has dissolved. Add peanut butter liquid to pan with capsicum (pepper). Simmer uncovered for 15 minutes.

To serve: Ladle into bowls and accompany with a basket of corn chips and a small bowl of sour cream.

Note: A little chilli powder to taste may be added with green capsicum (pepper).

Suitable to freeze.

SERVES 6

HEALTHY PUMPKIN SOUP

1 kg (2 lb) pumpkin

1 large potato, peeled and diced

1 large onion, diced

2 tomatoes, chopped

1 carrot, scraped and diced

1 stick celery, diced

1.5 litres (48 fl oz) chicken stock

1 tablespoon chopped fresh parsley

60 g (2 oz) uncooked rice

1 bay leaf

½ teaspoon chopped fresh oregano

slices of toast cut into triangles, to garnish

Cut pumpkin into wedges, remove membrane, peel and dice. Place in a deep pan with remaining ingredients. Cover and bring to the boil, then simmer for 40 minutes, stirring occasionally to prevent rice sticking. Remove bay leaf.

To serve: Ladle into bowls and garnish with triangles of toast.

Variation: Substitute 310 g (10 oz) can red, kidney or soy beans, drained and rinsed instead of rice.

Suitable to freeze.

SERVES 10

SERVING SOUP

For a quick meal, serve a hearty soup in a large mug, on a saucer with a spoon or serve soup in a bowl placed on a larger plate. This makes for easy handling.

ZUCCHINI (COURGETTE) AND TOMATO CHILLED SOUP

A wonderful soup for a hot summer day.

20 g (½ oz) butter

1 large onion, sliced

8 medium zucchini (courgettes) sliced

375 g (12 oz) can tomato purée

4 fresh basil leaves, chopped

2 cups (500 ml/16 fl oz) water

3 beef or vegetable stock cubes

natural yoghurt, to garnish

1 red tomato, very finely chopped, to garnish

Melt butter and gently fry onion until transparent, add zucchini (courgette), tomato purée, basil, water and stock cubes. Cover and bring to the boil. Simmer for 10 minutes. Cool slightly. Blend or push through strainer until smooth. Chill thoroughly before serving.

To Serve: Place in a large tureen and let guests help themselves to garnishes or ladle into bowls and swirl a little yoghurt in centre of soup, sprinkle finely chopped tomato on top.

Note: Soup can be served hot.

Suitable to freeze (without garnishes).

SERVES 6

CHILLED CUCUMBER SOUP

A delicate and sophisticated soup.

20 g (½ oz) butter

1 medium onion, sliced finely

3 large cucumbers

3 cups (750 ml/24 fl oz) water

3 chicken stock cubes

1 medium potato, peeled and diced

1 cup (250 ml/8 fl oz) thick cream or natural yoghurt

drop of green food colouring, optional

6 sprigs fresh mint, to garnish (these can be frozen in ice cubes if desired)

Heat butter in a saucepan and lightly fry onion. Trim ends from cucumbers, cut in half, scrape out and discard seeds. Chop cucumbers, add to onion and gently fry for 2 minutes. Add water, stock cubes and potato. Cover, bring to the boil. Simmer for 40 minutes. Blend or push through a sieve until smooth. Stir in cream or yoghurt and food colouring if desired.

Chill thoroughly before serving.

To Serve: Ladle into glass bowls and garnish with minted ice cube.

Variation: If serving this soup hot, add 1 cooked pork fillet, sliced into thin strips and 1 tablespoon light soy sauce.

Cream or yoghurt may be omitted.

Not suitable to freeze.

SERVES 6

EXOTIC CURRY AND COCONUT SOUP

500 g (1 lb) pumpkin

20 g (½ oz) butter

1 medium onion, sliced

1 medium potato, peeled and sliced

2 cups (500 ml/16 fl oz) chicken stock

1 cup (250 ml/8 fl oz) coconut cream (see Note)

1 teaspoon curry powder

½ teaspoon freshly crushed ginger

natural yoghurt, to garnish

shredded coconut, to garnish

packet of pappadums (cooked according to directions on packet), to garnish

Cut pumpkin into wedges, peel then remove membrane. Melt butter in a deep pan, gently fry onion until transparent. Add potato, pumpkin, stock, coconut cream, curry and ginger. Cover, bring to the boil then simmer for 30 minutes. Cool slightly. Blend or push through a sieve until smooth.

To Serve: Reheat, ladle into bowls, top with a swirl of yoghurt and sprinkle with coconut. Serve with pappadums.

Note: If commercial coconut cream is not available, place 1 cup (90 g/3 oz) desiccated coconut in a bowl. Pour 1½ cups (375 ml/ 12 fl oz) boiling water over and stand for 30 minutes. Strain, retaining liquid and squeeze coconut to remove all liquid, then discard coconut. Refrigerate and use within 24 hours.

Suitable to freeze (without yoghurt and garnishes).

SERVES 6

Char Grilled Octopus with Pumpkin Seed Sauce (page 25), Exotic Curry and Coconut Soup (recipe above)

BLOSSOM FLOWER SOUP

50 squash or zucchini (courgette) flowers

60 g (2 oz) butter

8 stalks garlic chives or shallots (spring onions), finely chopped

3 cups (750 ml/24 fl oz) chicken stock

½ teaspoon sugar

1 tablespoon lime juice

2 tablespoons chopped fresh coriander

½ cup (125 ml/4 fl oz) cream

extra chives, to garnish

sippets (see soup accompaniments page 19), to garnish

Chop flowers and wash. Melt butter in a deep pan and gently fry garlic chives or shallots for 1 minute. Add all remaining ingredients except cream. Cover, bring to boil then simmer for 15 minutes. Cool slightly. Blend until smooth.

To Serve: Reheat adding cream, do not boil. Ladle into bowls and garnish with finely chopped chives and sippets.

Suitable to freeze (without cream and garnish).

SERVES 6

OYSTER SOUP

250 g (8 oz) pumpkin, peeled

20 g (½ oz) butter

2 leeks (use white part only), diced

1 medium potato peeled and sliced

1 cup (250 ml/8 fl oz) chicken stock

1 bottle oysters (approximately 24 oysters)

1 tablespoon dry sherry

300 ml (10 fl oz) cream

1 small leek, extra, to garnish

freshly ground black pepper, to garnish

Cut pumpkin into wedges, remove membrane. Melt butter, gently fry leek for 30 seconds in a deep pan. Add pumpkin, potato and stock. Drain oysters and retain liquid, making oyster liquid up to 1 cup (250 ml/8 fl oz) with extra water, add to pan. Refrigerate oysters. Cover soup, bring to boil and simmer for 30 minutes. Cool slightly, add oysters (see Note), blend or push through sieve until smooth.

To Serve: Reheat soup with cream and sherry but do not boil. Chop extra leek very finely, sprinkle over the soup. with a little pepper.

Note: Oysters may be left whole, and added just before serving, as overheating oysters can cause them to toughen.

Not suitable to freeze.

SERVES 6

CRISP PASTRY

When totally covering soup with pastry, make a small hole in centre to allow steam to escape, keeping pastry crisp

---

PASTRY LIDS

Pastry Lids are an interesting variation for both Oyster Soup and Prawn Bisque.

6 individual ovenproof bowls two-thirds filled with Oyster Soup or Prawn Bisque

2 sheets ready-made puff pastry

1 tablespoon milk

1 egg, beaten

Preheat oven to 200°C (400°F).

Cut circles of pastry large enough to cover rim of soup bowls. Grease rims of bowls to grip pastry. Carefully place pastry over bowls of soup. Press to secure to rim. Mix milk and egg together, brush pastry with egg mixture, make a small hole in centre of pastry lids. Bake for 15 minutes until pastry rises and is golden.

MAKES 6

PRAWN (SHRIMP) BISQUE

500 g (16 oz) green prawns (shrimps)

2 cups (500 ml/16 fl oz) water

2 cups (500 ml/16 fl oz) chicken stock

250 g (8 oz) pumpkin, peeled, membrane removed, sliced

1 medium onion, sliced

1 stick celery, diced

1 small carrot scraped and diced

2 bay leaves

60 g (2 oz) tomato paste

½ cup (125 ml/4 fl oz) dry white wine

½ cup (125 ml/4 fl oz) cream

6 extra prawns, to garnish

freshly ground black pepper

VARIATION

Use pasta instead of a pastry lid.

150 g (5 oz) dry vermicelli or linguini pasta

boiling water

1 teaspoon oil

Shell and devein prawns (shrimps). Refrigerate. Place shells and heads in a pan with the water. Bring to the boil and simmer for 20 minutes. Strain liquid, retaining stock but discarding shells. Add chicken stock to prawn (shrimp) liquid to make 3 cups (750 ml/24 fl oz) stock (add extra water if not sufficient liquid). Place combined stock in a deep pan with all ingredients except prawns (shrimps), pasta and oil (if using pasta instead of pastry), cream and extra prawns (shrimps). Bring to boil, cover and simmer for 30 minutes. Add prawns (shrimps) and gently cook for a further 2 minutes.

Remove prawns (shrimps) for garnish and refrigerate until ready to serve.

If using pasta instead of a pastry lid, bring a saucepan of water to the boil, add the oil. Add the pasta and cook for 5 minutes. Drain.

Cool soup slightly, remove bay leaves, blend until smooth or push through sieve. Add cooked pasta, if using. Stir in cream.

To serve: Ladle bisque into bowls, garnish with extra prawn (shrimp).

Not suitable to freeze.

SERVES 6

OXTAIL POTAGE

1 oxtail, cut through joints and trimmed of excess fat

1 onion, diced

1 clove garlic, crushed

2 stalks celery, diced

1 carrot, scraped and diced

pinch of sugar

2 zucchini (courgette) trimmed and diced

3 cups (750 ml/24 fl oz) beef stock

grated Parmesan cheese, to garnish

dumplings, to garnish (see recipe this page)

Place all ingredients (except cheese and dumplings) in a deep pan, Cover, bring to boil then simmer slowly for 3 to 4 hours, or until meat falls from bone. Remove bones. Chill soup until fat has congealed on surface, then skim off the fat.

To Serve: Reheat soup to boiling point, add dumplings and follow instructions in Dumpling recipe. Ladle into bowls and sprinkle with grated Parmesan cheese.

This soup is ideal to cook in a pressure cooker. Follow recipe and pressure cook for 1½ hours. Cool before removing lid.

Suitable to freeze without dumplings and cheese.

SERVES 6

DUMPLINGS

250 g (8 oz) self-raising flour

pinch of salt

90 g (3 oz) butter

1 tablespoon chopped fresh parsley

cold water

extra flour

Place flour in a bowl, add salt, rub in butter with fingertips until mixture resembles fine breadcrumbs. Add parsley. With a knife, stir in water, a little at a time, until mixture has combined to form a soft ball. Sprinkle greaseproof paper with a little extra flour. Turn mixture out onto the floured paper and knead to form a smooth ball. Cut into 6 large or 12 small balls.

When soup is boiling, drop dumplings into soup, cook uncovered for 10 minutes. Cover and cook for a further 10 minutes.

Serve immediately with soup.

Variation: Add 1 tablespoon grated cheese to the flour mixture.

SERVES 6

FREEZING HINTS

Dumplings can be frozen uncooked. When cooking, do not defrost but allow extra minutes to cook in soup.

ACCOMPANIMENTS FOR SOUPS

CROUTONS: Small cubes of bread, brushed with oil, then fried or baked until crisp. Cool thoroughly, then store in an airtight container in a cool place for up to four weeks.

SIPPETS: Toast bread, remove all crusts, cut into small cubes. Will only keep two days.

PASTRY CROUTONS: Use one sheet of ready-made puff pastry, cut out shapes, brush with milk then bake in a hot oven until golden. Float on top of soup. Use within two days.

HALLOWE'EN SURPRISE

- *6 small golden nugget pumpkins, washed*
- *6 tablespoons warm water*
- *1 orange*
- *125 g (4 oz) pumpkin, extra, peeled, membrane removed*
- *1 medium onion, sliced*
- *1 medium potato, peeled and sliced*
- *30 g (1 oz) butter*
- *pinch salt*
- *2 teaspoons brown sugar*
- *2½ cups (600 ml/20 fl oz) strong chicken stock (see Note 1)*
- *½ cup (125 ml/4 fl oz) cream*
- *extra orange, to garnish (see Note 2)*
- *chopped parsley to garnish*

Preheat oven to 180°C (350°F).

Slice top from each golden nugget pumpkin and scoop out seeds. Pour 1 tablespoon water into each pumpkin. Bake in oven until insides are tender (or microwave on HIGH for 15 minutes). Cool pumpkins slightly, drain, scoop out flesh and retain. Place shells into individual serving dishes.

Peel orange very thinly, removing any white pith from rind, place rind into a deep pan. Peel white pith from orange and discard. Break the orange into segments, place in pan with orange rind, extra pumpkin, onion, potato, butter, salt, sugar and stock. Cover and bring to the boil. Simmer for 30 minutes. Add all golden nugget pumpkin flesh to pan, simmer a further 10 minutes.

Cool soup before blending or pushing through sieve.

To serve: Add cream and gently reheat. Spoon into pumpkin shells, garnish with orange slices and parsley.

Note 1: To make strong stock, add 5 stock cubes to 2½ cups water.

Note 2: Cut ends from extra orange. Slice into 6 rounds, carefully cut from rind almost to centre of each orange slice, twist and place on rim of each pumpkin shell bowl with a sprinkle of parsley over the orange slice.

Suitable to freeze (without cream or garnishes).

SERVES 6

GOLDEN PECAN NUT SOUP

A perfect dinner party soup. This soup has a strong nutty flavour, if desired the quantity of nuts may be decreased according to taste.

- *500 g (1 lb) pumpkin*
- *20 g (½ oz) butter*
- *1 medium onion*
- *3 cups (750 ml/24 fl oz) chicken stock*
- *125 g (4 oz) shelled pecan nuts*
- *sour cream, to garnish*
- *crushed pecan nuts to garnish*

Cut pumpkin into wedges, peel and remove membrane. Melt butter in a deep pan, fry onion until transparent. Add pumpkin, stock and nuts. Cover, bring to the boil and simmer for 30 minutes. Cool before blending or pushing through a sieve.

To serve: Reheat soup, ladle into bowls add a swirl of sour cream, top with crushed nuts.

Suitable to freeze (without garnishes).

Note: This soup is best made the day before use.

SERVES 6

Golden Pecan Nut Soup (recipe above), Crab Puffs (page 23)

Tempting Savouries For The Drinks Platter

MUSHROOMS BLUE

12 tiny mushrooms, wiped

1 tablespoon melted butter
or olive oil

2 tablespoons blue-vein cheese,
or cream cheese if preferred

½ cup mashed pumpkin

1 medium potato, cooked and
mashed

milk, warmed

2 rashers bacon

Preheat oven to 180°C (350°F).

Remove stalks from mushroom caps by twisting them. (These can be reserved for use later in soups and other dishes.) Brush mushrooms all over with butter or oil, place on oven tray or microwave safe plate. Place a small amount of cheese in base of mushroom caps.

Combine mashed pumpkin, potato and sufficient milk to form a soft, thick mixture. Place in a piping bag with a star nozzle. Pipe into cap or place spoonfuls in cap and mark with a fork.

Remove rind from bacon, cut into 24 fine strips. Place two strips, criss-crossed over filling in caps.

Heat in oven for 10 minutes (or microwave, on HIGH for 4 minutes).

Serve hot as a pre-dinner savoury.

MAKES 12

TOASTED CHILLI SEEDS

20 g (½ oz) butter
or 1 tablespoon of oil

60 g (2 oz) pumpkin seeds (keep
washed and dried pumpkin
seeds in the refrigerator until
you have sufficient)

equal amounts of salt and chilli
powder

Preheat oven 180°C (350°F).

Place butter or oil in pan, add seeds and roast in oven for 20 minutes, tossing twice. Cool. Combine salt and chilli powder, sprinkle over seeds.

Serve with drinks.

Will keep in an airtight container for 2 weeks.

PIPED EGGS

6 hard-boiled eggs

½ cup mashed pumpkin

1 shallot (spring onion), finely
diced

1 tablespoon tomato sauce

dash of Tabasco sauce

Shell eggs, cut in half lengthwise and carefully scoop out yolks. Mash yolks with pumpkin, shallot and sauces. (If a little thick, add a drop of warm milk.) Place in piping bag

fitted with a star nozzle, pipe mixture back into egg white halves (or spoon mixture into halves and mark with a fork).

Serve as a pre-dinner snack.

Can be made 12 hours ahead. Cover and refrigerate until needed.

MAKES 12

ALMOND CRUSTED BALLS

250 g (8 oz) tasty cheese, grated

½ cup mashed pumpkin

2 tablespoons plain flour

1 tablespoon finely chopped
garlic chives (or parsley
or nutmeg)

1 egg white, stiffly whisked

125 g (4 oz) blanched flaked
almonds

oil for deep frying

Combine, cheese, pumpkin, flour, garlic chives (or parsley or nutmeg) and egg white together. Mould small spoonfuls with hands to form balls. Roll in almonds. Refrigerate for 1 hour. Drop into hot oil, cook only until golden brown, drain.

Serve immediately.

Suitable to freeze. Cook while still frozen.

MAKES 12

CRAB PUFFS

*170 g (6 oz) can crab meat
or fresh crab meat*

½ cup mashed pumpkin

*½ teaspoon Chinese five spice
powder*

*2.5 cm (1 in) slice fresh
ginger, grated or crushed
or 1 teaspoon chilli honey
sauce*

2 sheets ready-made puff pastry

egg yolk

1 tablespoon milk

oil for deep frying

Drain crab meat and chop finely.
Add to pumpkin, mix in Chinese
five spice powder and ginger. Cut
each pastry sheet into 9 squares.
Place a spoonful of mixture into the
centre of each pastry square, brush
edges with combined egg yolk and
milk. Fold pastry to form a
triangle, pinch edges together to
form a decorative edge. Refrigerate
1 hour or more.

Heat oil, deep fry pastries until
golden brown. If preferred, puffs
can be brushed with egg and milk
and baked in a hot oven for 15 to
20 minutes.

Serve hot.

These can be made several weeks
ahead and frozen until ready to
cook.

Variation: Substitute canned red
salmon for crab meat.

MAKES 18

CRUNCHY MEAT BALLS WITH YOGHURT SAUCE

1 tablespoon butter or oil

1 onion, finely diced

60 g (2 oz) pinenuts

*500 g (16 oz) lean hamburger
mince*

½ cup mashed pumpkin

125 ml (4 fl oz) thick cream

1 egg, beaten

60 g (2 oz) currants

oil for deep frying

YOGHURT SAUCE

*200 g (6½ oz) carton natural
yoghurt*

*1 tablespoon finely chopped
fresh basil leaves*

Heat butter or oil in a pan and fry
onion and pinenuts until onions are
transparent. Drain. Combine all
ingredients. Form into small balls,
refrigerate for 1 hour or until ready
to cook. Heat oil in a large pan and
deep fry balls for 5 minutes until
golden and cooked. Drain on
absorbent paper towels.

To Prepare Yoghurt Sauce:
Combine ingredients.

Serve with a bowl of yoghurt sauce
for dipping.

Balls can prepared and frozen until
ready to use.

Variation: Substitute 500 g (16 oz)
cooked and flaked white fish for
hamburger mince.

MAKES ABOUT 16

ZUCCHINI (COURGETTE) ROUNDS WITH SMOKED SALMON

Best served the day the rounds
are baked.

250 g (8 oz) plain flour

1 teaspoon baking powder

pinch of salt

1 egg, beaten

*2 zucchinis (courgettes), cooked
and mashed*

milk

extra flour

TOPPING

softened cream cheese

smoked salmon

black caviar

sprigs of fresh dill, to garnish

Preheat oven to 200°C (400°F).

Sift flour, baking powder and salt
into a bowl. Using a knife, cut the
egg into the flour. Cut in mashed
zucchini (courgette), and sufficient
milk to make into a soft ball. Flour
a sheet of greaseproof paper, turn
out dough, knead lightly to make
into a smooth ball. Roll out to a
thickness of 5 cm (2 in), cut 2 cm
(¾ in) rounds with a small scone
cutter. Place on a greased oven
tray, brush with milk, bake for
10 to 12 minutes Cool.

To serve: Split rounds in half,
spread with soft cream cheese and
top with a small roll of smoked
salmon and a little caviar.

Garnish with a sprig of dill.

MAKES 24

To Prepare Risotto: Place rice and stock in a pan and simmer, uncovered for 10 minutes. Pour in half of the champagne, stir with a metal spoon. Simmer for 5 minutes more. Add remaining champagne. Stir rice until liquid is absorbed. The rice should be soft and moist. Add butter and parsley (if using).

To Cook in a Microwave: Place stock and rice in a deep covered container. Cook on HIGH for 5 minutes, add champagne, cook a further 10 minutes on HIGH or until all liquid is absorbed. Stir in butter and parsley (if using).

To Prepare Blossoms: Wash flowers gently. Allow to dry.

Prick eggplant (aubergine) once with fork and place in boiling salted water, simmer approximately 20 minutes or until skin is soft. Drain and cool. Gently fry onion in ½ tablespoon oil until transparent. Add tomatoes and simmer until very soft.

Cut cooked eggplant (aubergine) in half, scoop out flesh and add to tomato mixture. Mash lightly with a fork, add sugar and chilli. Stand for 30 minutes to allow flavours to blend.

To Prepare in a Microwave: Pierce the skin of the eggplant (aubergine) and cook on HIGH for 5 minutes. Cool. Cook the onions and tomatoes in ½ tablespoon of oil on HIGH for 5 minutes.

Using a small spoon, fill flowers with mixture. Fold flower petals inwards and secure with a toothpick. Heat a little oil and sauté the garlic. Gently fry stuffed flowers for 30 seconds on each side. Drain on absorbent paper.

To serve: Place flowers on risotto, allowing 2 flowers per serve and sprinkle with pepper.

ZUCCHINI (COURGETTE) BLOSSOMS SERVED ON A CHAMPAGNE RISOTTO

Zucchini (Courgette) Blossoms served on a Champagne Risotto

RISOTTO

220 g (7 oz) raw short-grain rice

2 cups (500 ml/16 fl oz) chicken stock

1 cup (250 ml/8 fl oz) champagne

1 teaspoon butter

1 tablespoon finely chopped fresh parsley (optional)

freshly ground black pepper

BLOSSOMS

8 flowers (zucchini (courgette), marrow or pumpkin flowers may be used)

1 small or ½ a large eggplant (aubergine)

boiling salted water

½ tablespoon oil

1 onion, finely diced

2 tomatoes, peeled and finely diced

1 small red chilli, seeded and chopped finely

1 teaspoon sugar

1 clove garlic, crushed

oil for shallow frying

SERVES 6

POACHED SCALLOPS WITH PUMPKIN PUREE

12 scallops

½ cup (125 ml/4 fl oz) milk

1 tablespoon butter or oil

1 onion, finely chopped

4 snow peas to garnish

½ cup (125 ml/4 fl oz) champagne or chicken stock

½ cup mashed pumpkin

½ cup (125 ml/4 fl oz) cream

½ tablespoon finely chopped fresh basil

Place scallops in milk, marinate 30 to 60 minutes, then drain.

Heat butter or oil in a frying pan and gently fry onion and snow peas until onion is transparent. Remove snow peas, drain, add champagne or stock to onion, bring to boil.

Combine pumpkin, cream and basil in a heavy based pan, stir over heat until piping hot (or place in microwave dish and cook on HIGH for 2 minutes). Spoon a circle of purée onto two plates.

Remove stock from heat, add drained scallops, stand for no more than 30 seconds. Spoon 6 scallops into centre of purée and spoon a little stock over scallops.

To serve: Garnish with snow peas and serve immediately.

SERVES 2

CHAR GRILLED OCTOPUS WITH PUMPKIN SEED SAUCE ON A WARM SALAD

½ teaspoon salt

4 cups (1 litre/32 fl oz) water

juice ½ lemon

24 baby octopus, heads removed and washed

MARINADE

1 Spanish onion, finely chopped

10 fresh basil leaves, finely chopped

juice ½ lemon

60 ml (2 fl oz) balsamic vinegar

60 ml (2 fl oz) light olive oil

SAUCE

125 g (4 oz) pumpkin seeds, washed, dried

8 fresh basil leaves

½ cup (125 ml/4 fl oz) light sour cream

1 tablespoon light oil

1 tablespoon water

1 small onion, diced

WARM SALAD

1 zucchini (courgette), trimmed

1 stick celery

1 small carrot

1 tablespoon oil

To Prepare Marinade: Combine all marinade ingredients.

To Prepare Salad: Slice zucchini (courgette), celery and carrot into thin matchsticks (julienne). Place vegetables in bowl of cold water, until you are ready to cook the octopus. Drain vegetables and pat dry. Heat oil in heavy based pan. Fry vegetables for 2 minutes, stirring all the time, do not brown. Drain.

To Prepare Sauce: Place a heavy-based pan over heat, add pumpkin seeds and stir for 1 minute. Do not brown. Process seeds in a blender with basil leaves, cream, water, oil and onion. Alternatively you can grind seeds, basil and onion together, then add liquids and mix well with a mortar and pestle.

Push seed mixture through a fine sieve, discarding grains and leaving a smooth paste.

Re-heat sauce, stirring all the time as sauce will tend to stick to bottom of pan (or microwave on HIGH for 1 minute).

To Prepare Octopus: Place salt, water, lemon juice and octopus in a pan and bring to the boil. Simmer for 2 minutes, drain and place octopus in a bowl. Pour marinade over octopus. Cover, allow to marinate 2 hours at room temperature.

Drain octopus, place on a grill tray or barbecue and cook until lightly charred.

To Serve: Divide salad between 6 plates. Arrange 4 octopuses on top of each and spoon seed sauce over the top. Garnish with extra pumpkin seeds.

Variation: Substitute green prawns (shrimps) for octopus. Leave heads and shells on the prawns (shrimps). Do not pre-cook. Marinade, and grill prawns (shrimps), until pink. Serve the prawns (shrimps), whole with sauce on the warm salad.

SERVES 6

ENTREE

A French term meaning 'beginning'. On a formal dinner menu, it comes third, between soup and roast.

BLOSSOMS WITH MOUSSELINE SERVED WITH SAUCE VERTE

8 zucchini (courgette) or pumpkin
or marrow flowers, washed

MOUSSELINE

2 fillets white fish (skinned and
boned)

125 ml (4 fl oz) thickened cream

1 tablespoon finely chopped fresh
dill

1 egg white, stiffly whisked

SAUCE

warm salted water

4 leaves silverbeet (spinach)

4 leaves fresh basil

30 g (1 oz) pine nuts

250 ml (8 fl oz) mayonnaise

To Prepare Mousseline: Blend fish, cream and dill until mixture forms a thick liquid. Whisk in egg white. Refrigerate for 1 hour.

Preheat oven to 180°C (350°F).

To Prepare Blossoms: Fill flowers carefully with mousseline. Place filled flowers on a greased oven tray. Cover with greased aluminium foil. Bake for 10 minutes.

To Prepare Sauce: Soak silverbeet (spinach) in salted water for 3 minutes, drain. Bring a pan of water to the boil, add leaves and simmer for 5 minutes. Drain well. Place leaves, basil, pine nuts and mayonnaise in a blender or food processor and mix or process until liquid. Reheat sauce, but do not boil.

To serve: Place blossoms on four entrée plates, accompany blossoms with sauce.

SERVES 4

SOUFFLE OYSTERS

12 oysters, in shell, opened

2 or 3 zucchini (courgette),
cooked and mashed

1 tablespoon fresh rosemary,
finely chopped (or ½ teaspoon
ground)

2 egg whites stiffly beaten

Preheat oven to 180°C (350°F).

Place a baking dish with about 5 cm (2 in) of water on lowest shelf of oven. Arrange oysters, in their shells on a separate oven tray. Combine zucchini (courgette) and rosemary in a large bowl, lightly whisk in egg whites. Place one spoonful of mixture on top of each oyster, making sure the oyster is completely covered. Bake for 10 minutes, or until soufflé has risen and is slightly brown.

Serve as soon as they are cooked.

Variation: Add 1 tablespoon grated tasty cheese to the soufflé mixture.

SERVES 6

WHY A PAN OF WATER?

A pan of water placed in the oven when cooking a soufflé creates steam, which prevents the soufflé boiling and helps to make it lighter.

*Blossoms with Mousseline served with
Sauce Verte (recipe above),
Zucchini (Courgette) Rounds with
Smoked Salmon (page 23)*

Lunches, Brunches and Suppers

Whether a quick snack for lunch, a late, leisurely brunch or a complete meal, the following recipes will satisfy any appetite.

NOTE

- 500 g (16 oz) wedge of uncooked pumpkin with skin yields 1 cup of cooked and mashed pumpkin.

CHINESE OMELETTE

1 tablespoon oil

2 shallots (spring onions), thinly sliced

60 g (2 oz) mushrooms, sliced

1 stick celery, diced

1 zucchini (courgette) sliced very finely in julienne strips

8 eggs

250 g (8 oz) cooked shelled prawns (shrimps) or cooked diced chicken

SAUCE

1 tablespoon cornflour

1 teaspoon sugar

1 cup (250 ml/8 fl oz) water

1 chicken stock cube

1 tablespoon light soy sauce

bean or snow pea sprouts, to garnish

Heat oil in an omelette pan and lightly fry shallots, mushrooms, celery and zucchini (courgette), until just soft. Remove from pan, drain. Beat eggs and add the vegetables, prawns or chicken. Pour one quarter of the mixture into the pan. Stir until mixture is just starting to set, carefully turn over. Cook until set. Repeat, making four omelettes.

To Prepare Sauce: Combine cornflour and sugar in a pan. Stir in water, crumbled stock cube and soy sauce, stirring until smooth. Bring to the boil, stirring until sauce thickens.

Pictured on previous pages: Pasta with Pumpkin, Tomato and Bacon Sauce (page 33), Vegetable and Lamb Couscous (page 34), Scallops in Orange Butter (page 38)

To serve: Stack omelettes on a warm serving plate, pour the sauce over and garnish with sprouts. Cut into four wedges and serve immediately with salad.

SERVES 4

ZUCCHINI (COURGETTE) OMELETTE

¼ cup (60 ml/2 fl oz) light olive oil

1 large Spanish onion, finely sliced

5 zucchini (courgette)

2 tablespoons bottled Italian tomato pasta sauce or 1 peeled tomato, diced

freshly ground black pepper

6 eggs, separated

green salad, to serve

fresh crusty bread, to serve

Preheat oven to 180°C (350°F).

Heat oil in a pan and fry onion until transparent. Trim ends from zucchini (courgette) and slice thinly. Add to onion, fry until vegetables are lightly brown. Cool.

To Prepare in Microwave: Cook the prepared vegetables together on HIGH for 2 minutes. Cool.

Add tomato sauce or diced tomato and pepper to mixture, then stir in egg yolks.

Whisk whites until stiff and gently fold into mixture. Spoon into a greased 20 cm (8 in) cake tin. Bake for 30 minutes until set and lightly brown on top.

To serve: Turn out onto a plate, cut into wedges and serve with a green salad and crusty bread.

Variation: 60 g (2 oz) tasty grated cheese may be added to vegetable mixture.

Mash zucchini (courgette) and onion, to provide a smoother omelette.

SERVES 6

ZUCCHINI (COURGETTE) RELLENOS

6 large zucchini (courgette)

250 g (8 oz) frozen or fresh corn kernels

2 eggs, beaten

2 tablespoons milk

freshly ground black pepper

125 g (4 oz) grated tasty cheese

¾ cup thick tomato salsa (available in jars in supermarkets in mild, medium and hot flavours)

corn chips, to garnish

sour cream, to garnish

Preheat oven to 180°C (350°F).

Trim ends from zucchini (courgette) and cut in half, lengthwise. Scoop out seeds, leaving a shell. Place zucchini (courgette) shells (close together for support) in a greased baking dish.

Combine corn, eggs, milk and pepper. Place spoonfuls into shells (or blend corn mixture, to make a smooth texture and pour into shells). Top with cheese. Cover with greased aluminium foil. Bake for 45 minutes, or until zucchini (courgette) is soft. Spoon salsa over zucchini, bake uncovered for a further 10 minutes.

Serve hot with corn chips and sour cream on the side.

Variation: Substitute 250 g (8 oz) cooked mince steak for corn.

SERVES 6

Zucchini (Courgette) Rellenos (recipe above), Golden Nugget Pumpkin with Herbed Goat's Cheese Filling (page 39)

5 cups (1.25 litres/40 fl oz) water

1 teaspoon oil

pinch salt

250 g (8 oz) pasta (1 quantity)

Bring water to a rolling boil in a large saucepan and add oil and salt. Place pasta into boiling water and cook until 'al dente' or 'just tender to the bite'. Drain well and serve immediately with a sauce of your choice.

SERVES 6

ZUCCHINI (COURGETTE) AND GARLIC SAUCE

500 g (16 oz) zucchini (courgettes)

1 onion, finely chopped

2 tablespoons olive oil

1 tablespoon plain flour

3 cloves garlic, crushed

pinch of sugar

250 g (8 oz) mozzarella cheese, chopped

freshly ground black pepper

425 g (13½ oz) can tomatoes

1 tablespoon tomato paste

½ teaspoon ground thyme

½ teaspoon ground basil

1 quantity of cooked pasta (see recipe this page)

Trim ends from zucchini (courgette), slice finely. Lightly fry zucchini (courgette), and onion in heated oil. Stir in flour, garlic, sugar, chopped cheese and pepper, return to heat and stir for 30 seconds. Stir in liquid from tomatoes, mash tomatoes and add to vegetable mixture, with

Zucchini (Courgette) and Garlic Pasta Sauce (recipe above), Chicken and Pumpkin Risotto (page 34), Stuffed Cucumbers (page 42)

tomato paste and herbs. Return to heat and stir until boiling. Lower heat and simmer, stirring occasionally, for 15 minutes.

To Prepare in Microwave: Combine all ingredients, cook on HIGH for 2 minutes, and for a further 5 minutes on MEDIUM.

Pour over pasta and serve.

SERVES 6

PUMPKIN, TOMATO AND BACON SAUCE

1 tablespoon oil

4 rashers bacon, rind removed and diced

2 shallots (spring onions), diced

425 g (13½ oz) can tomatoes

2 celery stalks, diced

250 g (8 oz) wedge pumpkin, peeled and cubed

½ cup (125 ml/4 fl oz) water

1 chicken or vegetable stock cube

pinch of dried basil

1 clove garlic, crushed

pinch sugar

1 quantity of cooked pasta (see recipe this page)

Heat oil in a pan and fry bacon until bacon fat is clear. Add shallots and tomatoes, including the liquid, chopping the tomatoes roughly. Add all remaining ingredients. Bring to the boil and simmer for 30 minutes.

Serve hot over pasta.

SERVES 6

BITTER GARLIC

Adding a pinch of sugar to garlic and tomatoes prevents the garlic from giving the dish a slightly bitter taste.

MUSSEL AND ZUCCHINI (COURGETTE) SAUCE

500 g (16 oz) fresh mussels

1 tablespoon olive oil

3 shallots (spring onions), diced

2 cloves garlic, crushed

pinch of sugar

500 g (16 oz) zucchini (courgette), trimmed and diced

½ cup (125 ml/4 fl oz) white wine

1 tomato, peeled and diced

1 stick celery, diced

8 fresh basil leaves, chopped

½ cup (125 ml/4 fl oz) chicken stock

1 quantity cooked pasta (see recipe page 33)

Bring a large saucepan of water to the boil, add mussels. Remove mussels as shell lip opens (cooking longer will only toughen mussel). Discard any mussels which have not opened. Place cooked mussels in a bowl with a little of the water to keep moist. Cover.

Heat oil, fry shallots, add garlic, sugar, zucchini (courgette), wine, tomato, celery, basil and chicken stock. Bring to boil, simmer uncovered until mixture thickens. Add mussels in their shells.

Serve immediately over hot pasta.

Variation: Substitute 500 g (16 oz) green prawns for mussels (shell or cook whole in boiling water until pink).

SERVES 6

CHICKEN AND PUMPKIN RISOTTO

2½ cups (600 ml/20 fl oz) chicken stock

1 tablespoon light oil

1 onion, sliced

1 clove garlic, crushed

pinch sugar

220 g (7 oz) uncooked rice

2 cups pumpkin purée (see Note)

approximately 600 g (20 oz) cooked, diced chicken meat

chopped fresh parsley, to garnish

grated parmesan cheese, to garnish

Place stock in a pan, bring to boil and keep at simmering point. Heat oil in a deep pan. Fry onion, until transparent, add garlic, sugar and rice. Stir for 3 minutes. Pour 1 cup hot stock into rice mixture, stirring until rice absorbs liquid. Add another cup hot stock, stir until absorbed.

Add remaining stock. Allow to simmer until rice has totally absorbed all the liquid (it should still be "al dente"). Add pumpkin purée and chicken, stir until heated though.

Serve on individual plates, sprinkled with parsley and grated cheese.

Note: Cook pumpkin then blend or mash with a little milk to form a thick liquid.

SERVES 6

COUSCOUS

Couscous is a North African cereal, made from semolina and rolled into little pearls.

VEGETABLE AND LAMB COUSCOUS

4 tomatoes, peeled, diced or 425 g (16 oz) can tomatoes

2 onions, diced

375 g (12 oz) zucchini (courgettes) trimmed and sliced into thin rounds

1 potato, peeled and diced

2 carrots, scraped and diced

1 bunch parsley, stems removed

2 cups (500 ml/16 fl oz) chicken stock

1 kg (2 lb) cooked lamb, diced

Couscous

extra 2 cups (500 ml/16 fl oz) chicken stock

1 teaspoon butter

375 g (12 oz) couscous

To Prepare Broth: Combine all vegetables with parsley and stock. If using canned tomatoes, chop tomatoes, add liquid to chicken stock to make up to 2 cups. Bring to the boil, simmer 30 minutes. Add lamb, reheat for 10 minutes.

To Prepare Couscous: Bring extra stock to boil, add butter. Add couscous. Simmer 1 minute, stirring constantly. Remove from heat. Cover. Stand 20 minutes. If all liquid has not been absorbed, return to heat and stir until all liquid is absorbed.

To Serve: Divide couscous onto six individual plates, in a ring shape. Spoon vegetables and lamb in the centre and spoon lamb broth over.

SERVES 6

SPAGHETTI SQUASH WITH SAVOURY MINCE

1 vegetable spaghetti squash

500 g (16 oz) lean mince steak

1 onion, finely chopped

1 stick celery, diced

1 carrot, scraped and diced

1 teaspoon Worcestershire sauce

1 teaspoon tomato sauce

½ cup (125 ml/4 fl oz) water

Place squash in a large saucepan
of boiling water. Boil gently for
30 minutes.

Combine all other ingredients in a
pan. Cover, bring to boil. Simmer
for 45 minutes.

To Prepare in Microwave: Prick skin
once, cook on HIGH for 15 minutes.
Combine all other ingredients and
microwave on HIGH for 20 minutes
stirring once.

Cut spaghetti squash in half,
lengthwise and remove seeds. With a
fork, scrape out the strands and mix
with meat mixture. Reheat.

Serve either in the shell of the
spaghetti squash or on warmed
plates.

SERVES 4 TO 6

ZUCCHINI (COURGETTE) SOUFFLE WITH BACON SAUCE

40 g (1½ oz) butter

1 tablespoon plain flour

¾ cup (185 ml/6 fl oz) milk

4 eggs, separated

60 g (2 oz) grated tasty cheese

*3 zucchini (courgettes) trimmed,
cooked and mashed*

SAUCE

2 teaspoons olive oil

*3 rashers bacon, rind removed,
diced*

1 small onion, peeled and diced

1 tablespoon Worcestershire sauce

3 tablespoons tomato sauce

3 tablespoons water

1 chicken stock cube, crumbled

Preheat oven to 180°C (350°F).

Stand a greased soufflé dish in a
baking dish with 2.5 cm (1 in) warm
water.

Melt butter in a saucepan, stir in
flour, cook for 1 minute stirring
continuously. Remove from heat, stir
in milk. Return to heat, stir until
sauce boils and thickens. Remove
sauce from heat and beat in egg
yolks, cheese, and zucchini
(courgette).

Whisk egg whites until stiff, fold
into zucchini (courgette) mixture.
Carefully spoon into soufflé dish.
With a knife, cut a circle, 0.5 cm
(¼ in) into soufflé, 2.5 cm (1 in)
from rim of dish (this will form a
raised lid when cooked). Bake for
30 to 40 minutes, until soufflé has
risen and is lightly brown on top.

To Prepare Sauce: Heat oil and fry
bacon and onion until bacon fat is
clear. Add other ingredients and
bring to boil.

To Prepare in a Microwave: Cook
oil, onion and bacon on HIGH for
2 minutes then add other ingredients
and cook on HIGH a further
3 minutes.

Serve cooked soufflé immediately
accompanied by the hot bacon sauce.

SERVES 4 TO 6

Zucchini (Courgette) Gnocchi with Cheesy Sauce (recipe on opposite page)

ZUCCHINI (COURGETTE) GNOCCHI WITH CHEESY SAUCE

250 g (8 oz) zucchini (courgette)

60 g (2 oz) butter

pinch of salt

60 g (2 oz) plain flour or plain wholemeal flour

2 eggs, beaten

30 g (1 oz) tasty cheese, grated

2 cups (500 ml/16 fl oz) boiling water

1 chicken stock cube, crumbled

SAUCE

60 g (2 oz) butter

1 tablespoon plain flour

1 cup (250 ml/4 fl oz) milk

125 g (4 oz) ricotta

1 teaspoon dry mustard

shavings of parmesan cheese, to garnish

Trim ends from zucchini (courgette). Cook in boiling water until tender (or microwave with 2 teaspoons of water on HIGH for 8 to 10 minutes until tender. Drain in a colander and mash, allowing excess water to escape.

Bring ½ cup (125 ml/4 fl oz) of water to the boil with butter and salt. Remove from heat. Stir in flour with wooden spoon, return to a gentle heat and stir continuously until mixture leaves the sides of the pan. Cool slightly. Add eggs, beating well. Add mashed zucchini (courgette) and cheese and mix well.

Drop teaspoonfuls of mixture into boiling water with stock cube.

Simmer until gnocchi rises to the surface. Remove with a slotted spoon and place into a heat proof dish.

To Prepare Sauce: Melt butter in pan, stir in flour and cook for 1 minute. Remove from heat. Stir in milk. Return to heat, stir until sauce boils and thickens. To cook in a microwave, melt butter on HIGH for 1 minute, then stir in flour and milk. Cook on high for 2 minutes more.

Add cheese and mustard.

To Serve: Pour the cheesy sauce over gnocchi, top with shavings of parmesan cheese.

Variation: Substitute 250 g (8 oz) cooked mashed pumpkin for zucchini.

SERVES 4

PUMPKIN PARCELS

Preparing Small Pumpkins and Other Squash for Fillings

The glorious colours of the golden nugget pumpkin and scallop squash provide a perfect casing to fill with a variety of luscious stuffings. Serve them on their own, or as a side dish. On the following pages are a series of such recipes.

COOKING METHODS

Choose glossy skinned, well coloured, firm golden nuggets or squash. Wash, scrub any dirt from skins. Prick skin once.

TO BOIL: Place vegetables in a pan. Add hot water to half cover the vegetables. Bring to the boil. Simmer until skin is just tender. Drain well.

TO MICROWAVE: Place in a microwave oven and cook on HIGH for 5 minutes. If not tender, continue cooking and test every 3 minutes until skin is just tender.

PREPARATION

Cool, cut tops from vegetable, scoop out seeds. The flesh can then be carefully removed. If not

using immediately, stuff shell with paper towelling or aluminium foil to hold the shape (this is not necessary if flesh is not removed). This process can be done the day before required, although best results are achieved if they are used as soon as possible after cooking.

SCALLOPS IN ORANGE BUTTER

500 g (16 oz) scallops

milk, to cover scallops

4 shallots (spring onions), chopped finely

4 zucchini (courgette) or 4 scallop squash, cooked, flesh removed (see recipe page 37)

ORANGE BUTTER

juice of 2 oranges

125 g (4 oz) butter

Preheat oven to 180°C (350°F).

Peel rind from oranges and remove any pith. Cut rind into small, thin julienne strips to use as a garnish.

Cover scallops with milk, marinate 1 hour at a cool room temperature. Drain scallops, add shallots. Spoon into zucchini (courgette) or squash shells.

Place zucchini (courgette) or squash in a baking dish with 2.5 cm (1 in) water. Bake for 10 minutes or until hot (or microwave on HIGH for 3 minutes).

To Prepare Orange Butter: Place orange juice in a pan over heat. Bring to the boil. Whisk in butter, a little at a time and cook for 20 seconds. Cool slightly. Pour equal amounts over scallops. Bake for a further 5 minutes (or microwave on HIGH for 2 minutes). Serve immediately, topped with strips of orange rind.

SERVES 4

CHILLI

Both dried and fresh chilli should be handled with care, as chilli contains volatile oils which, if they come in contact with the eye, cause a burning sensation. Wear rubber gloves when seeding and chopping chillies.

CHILLI PUMPKIN RAGOUT

6 golden nugget pumpkins, flesh removed and mashed (see recipe page 37)

125 g (4 oz) sesame seeds

125 g (4 oz) flaked almonds

1 tablespoon light olive oil

1 Spanish onion, diced finely

2 cloves garlic, crushed

1 teaspoon finely chopped chilli

1 cup (250 ml/8 fl oz) tomato purée (sauce)

1 teaspoon ground cumin

1 teaspoon ground oregano

pinch of sugar

sour cream, to garnish

toasted almonds, to garnish (see Note)

Place shells on serving plates.

Dry fry sesame seeds and almonds until lightly brown. Process or grind in a food processor, or place in a clean plastic food storage bag and crush with rolling pin, until fine crumbs are achieved.

Heat oil and lightly fry onion, garlic and chilli. Add tomato purée, cumin, oregano, sugar and mashed pumpkin flesh. Bring to the boil, add crushed nuts. Simmer for 10 minutes.

To Serve: Spoon mixture into shells, swirl a little sour cream on top and sprinkle with extra toasted almonds.

Note: Dry fry extra almonds until lightly brown. Cool thoroughly, store in airtight container for several weeks.

SERVES 6

MADEIRA

Madeira is a fortified dessert wine. Originally from the Portuguese island of Madeira. It gives a full bodied flavour to brown sauces.

MADEIRA SAUTE KIDNEYS

6 golden nugget pumpkins or scallop squash shells, medium size (see recipe page 37)

6 veal or lamb kidneys

1 tablespoon vegetable oil or 20 g (½ oz) butter

1 Spanish onion, finely chopped

3 tablespoons madeira wine

2 tablespoons cream

Remove membrane, fat and tubes from kidneys, slice very finely. Heat oil or butter, lightly fry onion. Add kidneys and fry, stirring all the time, for 4 minutes. Pour in wine and allow to simmer for 1 minute more. Stir in cream. Spoon into pumpkin or squash shells.

Serve as a main course with salad and French fries or as an entrée dish served on a cup of lettuce.

SERVES 6

ZUCCHINI (COURGETTE) STUFFING FOR CHICKEN

1 chicken

4 zucchini (courgette), finely sliced

1 cup fresh breadcrumbs or cooked rice

4 mushrooms, finely sliced

1 onion, finely sliced

pinch of thyme, sage, and nutmeg

1 egg, beaten

Rinse chicken and dry well. Combine all remaining ingredients and use as a stuffing for chicken.

Variation: Zucchini (courgette) may be cooked and mashed if a softer stuffing is desired.

CHEESE CUSTARD

This dish can also be prepared in a microwave.

4 medium golden nuggets or scallop squash, flesh removed and retained (see recipe page 37)

2 teaspoons butter

milk

½ cup (125 ml/4 fl oz) cream or evaporated milk

2 eggs, beaten

60 g (2 oz) cottage cheese

6 leaves fresh marjoram, chopped

Preheat oven to 160°C (325°F).

Place a baking dish containing a little water on the bottom shelf of the oven. Place shells on a greased oven tray.

Mash flesh with butter and sufficient milk to make a smooth, soft mixture. Add all remaining ingredients and mix well. Spoon into shells. Bake for 15 minutes.

To Prepare in Microwave: Cook on High for 3 minutes, then on LOW for 6 minutes. Test to see if custard is firm, if not, cook another 1 minute. Test and cook until firm but do not allow to boil.

Serve as a side vegetable, or with a salad and crisp chips for lunch.

SERVES 4

CREAMY CHICKEN AND CORIANDER FILLING

Pictured on cover.

4 prepared golden nugget shells (see recipe page 37)

2 teaspoons oil

4 chicken breast fillets, cubed

1 tablespoon wholegrain mustard

⅓ cup (80 ml/2½ fl oz) dry white wine

¾ cup mayonnaise

2 tablespoons coriander leaves

freshly ground black pepper

Heat oil in a frying pan over moderate heat. Add chicken and gently fry for 5 minutes or until golden brown.

Add mustard and wine to pan and simmer for 5 minutes.

Stir through mayonnaise and coriander and cook for 1 minute.

Place filling into cooked golden nugget pumpkin shells. Sprinkle with black pepper and serve.

SERVES 4

HERBED GOAT'S CHEESE

125 g (4 oz) goat's cheese

¾ cup (185 ml/6 fl oz) olive oil

3 sprigs fresh thyme, chopped

6 leaves fresh basil, chopped

4 large prepared scallop squash or medium golden nugget pumpkins, flesh removed and retained, (see recipe page 37)

4 slices fresh bread, crusts removed

1 teaspoon dried thyme

Preheat oven to 180°C (350°F).

Place cheese in a bowl, cover with oil and fresh herbs and marinate for 4 hours. Drain oil from cheese, retaining oil. Mash cheese and herbs with flesh from squash. Place squash shells in a baking dish with a little water, spoon in cheese mixture.

Crumble fresh bread and mix with dried thyme. Add a little of the marinade oil to make a dough. Spread dough on top of stuffed shells. Bake for 10 minutes, uncovered.

Serve hot with a green salad.

Variation: Substitute any cream or cottage cheese for goat's cheese.

SERVES 4

SPINACH AND PINE NUTS

6 medium golden nugget pumpkins or 6 large scallop squash, flesh removed and mashed (see recipe page 37)

6 leaves spinach (silverbeet)

1 teaspoon salt

125 g (4 oz) plain yoghurt

60 g (2 oz) sultanas

1 clove garlic, crushed

30 g (1 oz) pine nuts

2 slices fresh bread, crusts removed, crumbled

Preheat oven to 180°C (350°F).

Cover spinach (silverbeet) leaves with warm water and salt, leave to soak for 5 minutes (this removes any grit or small insects). Shake leaves well. Chop finely. Place in a bowl and add boiling water to cover. Allow to stand a further 5 minutes. Drain well.

Combine, chopped spinach leaves, yoghurt, sultanas, garlic, pine nuts, bread crumbs and mashed flesh. Spoon equal amounts of filling into shells. Bake for 20 to 25 minutes.

Serve as an accompaniment to a meat dish or serve with salad.

SERVES 6

SMOKED TROUT WITH SORREL SAUCE

6 medium size prepared golden nuggets or 6 scallop squash (see Note), with flesh (see recipe page 37)

1 smoked trout (approximately 250 g/8 oz)

125 g (4 oz) cream cheese

1 egg

juice of ½ lemon

¼ cup (60 ml/2 fl oz) cream

SAUCE

20 g (½ oz) butter or 1 tablespoon light olive oil

1 leek, diced

2 cups fresh sorrel, chopped

1 cup (250 ml/8 fl oz) chicken stock

extra 20 g (½ oz) butter

1 tablespoon plain flour

¼ cup (60 ml/2 fl oz) thickened cream

4 thin slices lemon or lime, to garnish

6 sorrel leaves, to garnish, if desired

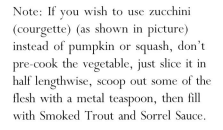

Note: If you wish to use zucchini (courgette) (as shown in picture) instead of pumpkin or squash, don't pre-cook the vegetable, just slice it in half lengthwise, scoop out some of the flesh with a metal teaspoon, then fill with Smoked Trout and Sorrel Sauce.

Preheat oven to 180°C (350°F).

Place pumpkin, squash or zucchini (courgette) shells in a baking dish with 2.5 cm (1 in) water.

Remove skin from trout, remove bones and flake fish. Place fish and all remaining ingredients in a blender or food processor. Blend or process until just combined. Spoon into prepared shells. Cover with aluminium foil. Bake for 35 to 40 minutes (20 minutes if using zucchini (courgette)) until firm.

To Prepare Sorrel Sauce: Heat butter or oil in a pan and lightly fry leek until soft. Add sorrel. Reduce heat, cook for 2 minutes. Add stock and bring to the boil. Simmer for 3 minutes. Blend or process until smooth.

Melt extra butter, stir in flour, stir for 30 seconds then remove from heat. Add sorrel and stock mixture. Stir until sauce boils. Remove from heat and stir in cream.

To Prepare in Microwave: Cook butter on HIGH for 1 minute, stir in flour and stock. Cook a further 2 minutes on HIGH. Stir in cream.

To Serve: Place fish filled pumpkin, squash or zucchini (courgette) shells on four individual entrée plates, pour a little sauce around each shell. Garnish with a twist of lemon or lime and a leaf of sorrel. Variation: Any fish may be used.

SERVES 6

Zucchini (Courgette) filled with Smoked Trout with Sorrel Sauce (recipe above), Mussel and Zucchini (Courgette) Pasta Sauce (page 34)

HIGH TOP

*2 medium golden nuggets or
scallop squash, flesh removed
(see recipe page 37)*

1 teaspoon dried thyme

20 g (½ oz) soft butter

1 tablespoon milk

3 eggs, separated

Preheat oven to 200°C (400°F).

Place a baking dish containing
2.5 cm (1 in) water on bottom shelf
of oven. Place pumpkin or squash
shells on a greased oven tray.

Mash pumpkin or squash flesh,
thyme, butter and milk together.
Heat until just starting to bubble,
remove from heat. Beat in egg yolks.
Whip whites until very stiff, fold
into mixture, spoon into shells. Bake
for 30 to 40 minutes until mixture is

*Zucchini (Courgette) Omelette (page 30),
High Top (recipe below)*

puffy and brown. Serve immediately
as a side dish to a main course, or as
an entrée.

Variation: 2 tablespoons grated tasty
cheese may be added to the heated
mixture. Stir until melted.

SERVES 2

BEANS 'N' CHILLI

This recipe can be made with or without the minced meat. It is pictured on the cover, without the meat.

1 marrow or 1 large golden nugget pumpkin, cooked (see recipe page 37)

310 g (10 oz) can kidney beans

1 tablespoon oil or 20 g (½ oz) butter

1 onion, sliced

400 g (13 oz) can tomatoes

500 g (16 oz) hamburger mince, optional

½ teaspoon chilli powder

tasty grated cheese, to garnish

Drain kidney beans, rinse with cold water, drain.

Heat oil or butter in a frying pan and lightly fry onion. Add can tomatoes, chopping tomatoes roughly. Stir in mince, beans and chilli. Bring to the boil, and simmer for 30 minutes.

To Serve: Fill marrow with mixture, then slice into thick slices or fill pumpkin with mixture and leave whole. Top with grated tasty cheese.

Note: This recipe can also be made without mince meat (see cover) making it a great vegetarian alternative.

SERVES 4

STUFFED CUCUMBERS

3 green cucumbers

salt

STUFFING

1 tablespoon light olive oil

1 clove garlic, crushed

1 onion, finely chopped

1 rasher bacon, rind removed, finely diced

3 mushrooms, finely diced

90 g (3 oz) rice, cooked in boiling water according to directions on packet

TOPPING

grated cheese

dried breadcrumbs

Cut cucumbers in half, lengthwise. Remove seeds, sprinkle with salt. Stand for 30 minutes. Drain.

Preheat oven to 200°C (400°F).

Heat oil in a frying pan and lightly fry garlic, onion and bacon, until the fat of the bacon is clear. Drain excess oil. Add mushrooms, stir over heat until tender. Add rice and mix well.

Fill centre of cucumbers with mixture, top with cheese and breadcrumbs.

Bake for 15 to 20 minutes until cheese has bubbled and browned.

Serve half a cucumber per serve as an accompaniment to a main course, or two halves with salad for a complete meal.

STUFFED MARROW

This recipe can be prepared in a microwave.

1 large marrow

1 tablespoon olive oil or 20 g (½ oz) butter

1 onion, sliced

500 g (16 oz) lean hamburger mince

1 tablespoon chopped fresh parsley

2 tablespoons tomato sauce

1 egg, beaten

2 slices fresh bread, crust removed, crumbled

Preheat oven to 180°C (350°F).

Cut one end from marrow, carefully scoop out seeds. Place marrow on a greased baking tray.

Heat oil or butter in a frying pan and lightly fry onion. Add remaining ingredients. Carefully spoon into centre of the marrow. Cover cut end of marrow with greased aluminium foil and bake 30 to 40 minutes until marrow skin is soft.

To Prepare in Microwave: Cover cut end with plastic wrap, place on plate, cook on HIGH for 5 minutes, then cook on MEDIUM for 15 minutes.

Remove aluminium foil or wrap.

Serve cut into slices, with cooked vegetables or salad.

SERVES 6

TUNA STUFFED CUCUMBERS

3 cucumbers, cut lengthwise, seeds removed

220 g (7 oz) can tuna

juice of 1 lemon

3 tablespoons mayonnaise

1 teaspoon Worcestershire sauce

1 tablespoon tomato sauce

Hollow cucumbers slightly with a metal teaspoon. Combine other ingredients in a bowl, mash to combine Spoon mixture into cucumbers. Chill thoroughly

Serve with a tossed salad.

SERVES 3

YEMISTA MARROW WITH A MINT GRAVY

This recipe is based on a tasty Greek dish and can be prepared in a microwave.

220 g (7 oz) short-grain rice

3 cups (750 ml/24 fl oz) chicken stock

1 large whole marrow

1 tablespoon oil or 20 g (½ oz) butter

1 large onion, sliced

500 g (16 oz) lamb mince

1 tomato, peeled and chopped

4 leaves fresh mint chopped

pinch of nutmeg

1 egg, beaten

GRAVY

1 tablespoon oil or 20 g (½ oz) butter

1 tablespoon plain flour

½ cup (125 ml/4 fl oz) beef stock

12 fresh mint leaves, crushed or chopped very finely

Preheat oven to 180°C (350°F).

Cut off one end of marrow, remove seeds. Place stock in a saucepan and bring to the boil. Add rice and simmer for 15 minutes, (or microwave on HIGH for 10 minutes). Drain.

Heat oil or butter in a frying pan and gently fry onion and lamb mince for 4 minutes, stirring constantly. Add tomato, mint, nutmeg, rice and egg. Spoon into marrow. Cover end with greased aluminium foil. Place on a greased oven tray. Bake for 1 hour.

To Prepare in Microwave: Cover end with plastic wrap. Cook on HIGH for 2 minutes then lower to MEDIUM for a further 10 minutes. Allow to cool slightly before removing from microwave.

To Prepare Gravy: Heat oil or butter in a saucepan, add flour, stir until it browns slightly. Add stock and mint, stir until mixture boils then allow to simmer until thick.

To serve: Cut marrow into thick slices, serve with gravy and a green vegetable.

SERVES 6

GRAPEFRUIT CHICKEN AND ALMONDS

1 marrow, washed, one end cut off, seeds removed.

60 g (2 oz) flaked almonds

1 large grapefruit

2 cups chicken, cooked and diced

½ cup (125 ml/4 fl oz) mayonnaise

125 g (4 oz) thick sour cream

3 sprigs fresh parsley

1 tablespoon finely chopped fresh chives

Preheat oven to 180°C (350°F).

Brown almond flakes by either stirring in a pan over heat or oven baking until just brown.

Peel grapefruit thickly to remove skin and pith. Break into segments then cut into small pieces.

Combine all ingredients and spoon into marrow. Wrap end of marrow in greased aluminium foil. Bake for 15 minutes.

To Prepare in Microwave: Cover end in plastic wrap, cook on HIGH for 3 minutes, then lower to MEDIUM and cook for a further 5 minutes.

Serve as a complete dish, with salad or French fries.

SERVES 6

ORIGIN OF MAYONNAISE

Mayonnaise was created by Napoleon's chef, in celebration of the capture of the island of Mahon.

STIR-FRY VEGETABLE FILLING

Pictured on cover.

4 prepared golden nugget pumpkin shells (see recipe page 37)

2 teaspoons sesame oil

1 red capsicum (pepper), sliced

1 green capsicum (pepper), sliced

2 zucchini (courgette), finely sliced

6 baby yellow squash, sliced

2 teaspoons lime juice

1 tablespoon soy sauce

1 tablespoon chopped lemon thyme

Heat oil in a frying pan over moderate heat. Add capsicums (peppers), zucchini and squash and stir fry for 3 minutes. Add lime juice, soy and thyme and cook for a further 2 minutes. Spoon the vegetables into 4 cooked golden nugget pumpkin shells and serve.

SERVES 4

Salads and Vegetable Accompaniments

Vegetables and salads can be meals in themselves or wonderful accessories to a meal. These tempting recipes emphasise the versatility of vegetables.

PUMPKIN PUREE

1 large butternut pumpkin

Cut pumpkin into four pieces, remove seeds. Place in a saucepan of boiling water, simmer until flesh is tender. Scoop out the flesh, discarding the skin. Process until smooth or mash and beat until smooth with 2 tablespoons of the cooking water to make into a thick, smooth mixture.

To Prepare in Microwave: Cut butternut in half, remove seeds. Microwave on HIGH for 10 minutes, test for tenderness. If necessary continue cooking for 5 minute intervals until flesh is tender. Stand 4 minutes before scooping out the flesh. Either blend, process or mash until smooth with a little water to make a thick, smooth mixture.

SERVES 6

ORANGE GINGER PUREE

juice of 1 orange

2.5 cm (1 in) slice fresh ginger, finely chopped

1 quantity of Pumpkin Purée (see recipe page 46)

Combine all ingredients. Serve with crumbed brains or whole baked fish.

Pictured on previous pages: Salad of Marrow Flowers (page 62), Ratatouille (page 51) served with Lamb Cutlets en Croute (page 46)

APPLE PUMPKIN PUREE

3 green apples

juice of ½ lemon

1 quantity of Pumpkin Purée (see recipe page 46)

Cut apples into quarters, peel and remove core. Place, with skins, in a pan of boiling water and boil gently until tender (or microwave on HIGH for 5 minutes). Drain, remove skins and discard, mash apples with lemon juice. Beat apple mixture into purée.

Serve with pork fillets, baked in herbs and sliced.

MINTED PUMPKIN PUREE

1 tablespoon oil or 20 g (½ oz) butter

1 onion, thinly sliced

8 fresh mint leaves, finely chopped

1 quantity of Pumpkin Purée (see recipe page 46)

Heat oil or butter in a frying pan and lightly fry onion. Add mint and stir for 30 seconds. Beat into pumpkin purée.

This is delicious served with Lamb Cutlets en Croute.

LAMB CUTLETS EN CROUTE

6 lamb cutlets, trimmed of excess fat

12 prunes, seeds removed

12 dried apricots

2 sheets ready-made puff pastry

1 egg yolk mixed with 1 tablespoon milk

Preheat oven to 200°C (400°F).

Flatten cutlets with a kitchen mallet or rolling pin. Holding the end of the bone, trim the meat up the bone with a sharp knife to cut the meat away from the bone. Then scrape the meat up to the large end of the cutlet, folding it back onto cutlet meat to leave the bone clean and all meat at the top.

Place 1 prune and 1 apricot on cutlet meat Place cutlet on pastry, cut around cutlet allowing pastry to fold around the shape, covering the meat on the cutlet completely, but allowing the bone to stay bare. Brush with combined egg and milk. Repeat with each cutlet. With remaining pastry, cut out little fancy shapes and arrange on cutlet pastry, securing with egg mixture. Brush all over pastry with egg mixture. Place on greased baking tray. Wrap bone in two layers of aluminium foil covering bone completely. Bake for 20 minutes until pastry is puffy and brown.

To Serve: Remove aluminium foil, serve on Minted Pumpkin Purée, with seasonal vegetables, or serve with Ratatouille.

Note: Cutlets can be frozen in the pastry case for up to 3 months. Glaze and bake whilst frozen.

SERVES 6

MARROW PUREE

1 large marrow

Cover with boiling water, simmer until tender. Cool, remove skin and seeds. Process or mash flesh until smooth, with a little of the cooking water.

To Prepare in Microwave: Cook on HIGH for 8 minutes, test for tenderness. If necessary, cook at 2 minute intervals until tender. Allow to stand for 3 minutes. Cut in half, remove seeds, scoop out flesh. Process or mash until smooth, adding a little water to make into a thick, smooth mixture.

SERVES 6

MARROW PUREE WITH HERBS

1 tablespoon oil

1 large onion, thinly sliced

1 bay leaf

½ teaspoon ground cumin

½ teaspoon ground coriander

1 clove garlic, crushed

1 teaspoon sugar

1 tablespoon tomato paste

1 quantity of Marrow Purée (see recipe page 46)

Heat oil, and fry onion until transparent. Add remaining ingredients, bring to the boil and simmer for 5 minutes. Remove bay leaf.

Serve with grilled meat, baked fish fillets, tuna cakes, freshly cooked mussels, lamb or beef curry.

ZUCCHINI (COURGETTE) PUREE

12 large zucchini (courgette)

Trim ends. Cover with boiling water simmer until tender. Cool. Cut in half, remove seeds, scoop out flesh. Process or mash until smooth, adding a little water to make into a thick, smooth mixture.

To Prepare in Microwave: Trim ends. Cook on HIGH for 8 minutes, test for tenderness. If necessary, cook at 2 minute intervals until tender. Allow to stand for 3 minutes.

SERVES 6

ROSEMARY ZUCCHINI (COURGETTE) PUREE

1 sprig of fresh rosemary, stem removed

1 quantity of Zucchini (Courgette) Purée (see recipe page 47)

Combine zucchini (courgette) purée with rosemary.

Serve with baked rack of lamb or veal.

CHOKO PUREE

6 chokos

Peel and seed choko. Cover with boiling water. Simmer until tender.

Mash or process with a little water to make a thick, smooth mixture.

To Prepare in Microwave: Peel and seed. Place in a dish with 1 tablespoon water, cook on HIGH for 8 minutes. Test for tenderness, if necessary cook at 2 minute intervals until tender.

SERVES 6

TANTALISING TOPPINGS

Here are some simple toppings to change pumpkin and squash into 'Cinderella at the ball' vegetables. No quantities are given, so add toppings to taste.

- Cube cooked pumpkin, drizzle with honey.

- Sprinkle cooked pumpkin with a little orange juice and freshly ground black pepper.

- Sprinkle sliced, raw pumpkin with tomato sauce and bake.

- Mash cooked pumpkin with natural yoghurt to make it creamy and sprinkle with ground nutmeg.

- Mash cooked pumpkin with cream to make it smooth and sprinkle with sultanas.

- Cook diced pumpkin with peeled and diced apple, sprinkle with caraway seeds.

- Mash pumpkin (approximately 2 cups), with 1 egg and sufficient plain flour to make a firm dough and pipe with bag and large star nozzle onto greased oven tray to form a swirl. Bake until lightly brown.

- Mash cooked chokos with finely chopped ginger and a little lemon juice.

- Peel, halve and seed choko. Cook, then fill hollow with sour cream, sprinkle with grated cheese and grill to brown the cheese.

- Mash cooked pumpkin, choko or marrows with curry powder and butter.

- Cook zucchini (courgette), slice and combine with sliced cooked onion and fresh basil.

- Toss cooked, diced zucchini (courgette) with crushed garlic and sesame seeds.

CURRIED CHOKO PUREE

1 tablespoon oil

1 onion, sliced

1 teaspoon curry powder

2 teaspoons coconut cream

6 water chestnuts, chopped

1 quantity of Choko Purée
(see recipe page 47)

Heat oil and gently fry onion, stir in curry powder, coconut cream, water chestnuts and purée. Serve hot.

STORING WATER CHESTNUTS

Water chestnuts can be stored for up to two months, covered with water in a screw top jar. Store in refrigerator. Change water once a week.

CUCUMBER SAMBAL

Serve as an accompaniment to curries.

2 cucumbers, peeled and sliced very thinly

salt

250 g (8 oz) natural yoghurt or sour cream

1 clove garlic, crushed

squeeze lemon or lime juice

Sprinkle cucumbers with salt, stand 30 minutes. Rinse and drain. Mix remaining ingredients together, add cucumbers. Chill thoroughly before serving.

STIR-FRYING

Stir-frying is a Chinese method of quick cooking in a wok or heavy based frypan. The vegetables are thinly sliced and cooked in a minimum of oil, retaining most of the vitamins and minerals.

MIXED STIR-FRY

1 carrot, scraped

4 shallots (spring onions)

½ red capsicum (pepper)

1 stick celery

2 mushrooms

1 zucchini (courgette), ends trimmed

18 snow peas or green beans, whole

1 tablespoon light vegetable or nut oil

1 clove garlic, crushed

2.5 cm (1 in) cube fresh ginger, finely chopped

1 tablespoon pine nuts

1 tablespoon oil, extra

Wash, and diagonally slice, very thinly, the carrot, shallot, capsicum (pepper), celery, mushrooms and zucchini (courgette). Trim snow peas or green beans.

Heat oil in a wok or heavy based frying pan and fry garlic, ginger and pine nuts until lightly brown. Drain and reserve. Heat extra oil, stir-fry snow peas or beans for 2 minutes, add remaining vegetables, stir-fry for 3 minutes. Add pine nut mixture and serve immediately.

SERVES 4

Curried Choko Purée served with grilled zucchini (courgette) (recipe above), Cucumber Florentine (page 54)

SAUTE ZUCCHINI (COURGETTE)

1 tablespoon oil

6 zucchini (courgettes) trimmed and thinly sliced

1 tomato peeled and thinly sliced

1 onion cut into thin rounds

2 tablespoons fresh chopped coriander

squeeze of fresh lemon or lime juice

Heat oil in a wok or heavy based frying pan and stir-fry vegetables for 5 minutes. Add coriander and juice. Serve immediately.

SERVES 6

BUTTON SQUASH

To Prepare on Hotplate: Wash button squash well and cook by steaming or gently boiling.

To Prepare in Microwave: Cook on HIGH for 4 minutes. Stand and test for tenderness. If required, cook for a further 1 minute on HIGH. If overcooked the button squash will toughen and shrink.

Remove centre of the cooked button squash with an apple corer or knife and fill with one of the following:

- finely chopped cooked tomato and onion

- finely chopped cooked tomato and celery

- finely chopped cooked meats

- any leftover meats or vegetables, finely chopped

- grated cheese

- toasted pine nuts

- finely chopped cooked mushrooms mixed with sour cream.

CAPSICUM (PEPPER) AND PUMPKIN

500 g (16 oz) pumpkin, peeled, seeds removed

1 red capsicum (pepper) seeds removed, sliced

1 green capsicum (pepper) seeds removed, sliced

1 onion, thinly sliced

3 cloves garlic, crushed

1 teaspoon caraway seeds

Cut pumpkin into 2.5 cm (1 in) cubes. Steam or boil until almost tender. Add capsicum (pepper), onion and garlic. Cook for a further 5 minutes, drain (or microwave pumpkin on HIGH for 5 minutes, add capsicum, onion and garlic and cook on HIGH for 3 minutes).

Stir in caraway seeds, reheat.

Serve with grilled steak, chops or sausages.

Variation: Substitute marrow, squash or choko for pumpkin, or substitute 1 teaspoon tarragon in place of caraway seeds.

SERVES 6

CHOKOS

6 chokos, peeled, seeds removed
butter
freshly ground black pepper

Steam, boil or microwave chokos until tender. Drain, mash with butter and a dash of pepper.

SERVES 6

HERBS

Always chop fresh herbs before washing.

SQUASH WITH DILL BUTTER

1 large squash or marrow

20 g (½ oz) butter or 1 tablespoon oil

1 tablespoon plain flour

1 cup (250 ml/8 fl oz) chicken stock

1 small bunch fresh dill, chopped

juice of ½ lemon

freshly ground black pepper

Peel marrow or squash and remove seeds with a spoon. Cut flesh into cubes. Steam or boil until just tender (or microwave on HIGH for 2 minutes). Drain.

Heat oil in a saucepan, add flour, stir for 30 seconds then remove from heat. Stir in stock. Return to heat, bring to the boil, stirring constantly (or to microwave, heat oil on HIGH for 30 seconds, stir in flour, stir in stock and cook on HIGH for 2 minutes). Add dill, lemon juice and pepper to taste.

Add cooked vegetable cubes to sauce. Stir until reheated, (or microwave on HIGH for 2 minutes).

Serve immediately with grilled meat, fish or chicken.

Variation: Substitute peeled chokos for marrow or squash.

SERVES 6

RATATOUILLE

- *1 eggplant (aubergine) approximately 500 g (16 oz)*
- *1 tablespoon oil*
- *1 onion, diced*
- *1 stick celery, sliced*
- *1 zucchini (courgette) thinly sliced in rounds*
- *1 tomato, peeled and chopped*
- *1 clove garlic, crushed*
- *1 teaspoon sugar*
- *½ banana, peeled and sliced thinly into rounds*
- *grated tasty cheese*
- *brown breadcrumbs*

Place eggplant (aubergine) into a pan of boiling water and cook for 25 minutes or steam until tender (or, to cook in microwave, prick skin once, cook on HIGH for 10 minutes). Cool, cut in half, remove and retain flesh. Place eggplant (aubergine) shells on griller tray.

Heat oil in a frying pan and fry onion until transparent. Add celery, zucchini, tomato, garlic and sugar, simmer until vegetables are just tender, (or combine, oil, onion, celery, tomato, garlic, and sugar together and microwave on HIGH for 4 minutes).

Add eggplant (aubergine) flesh and banana to vegetables, and stir over heat until hot, (microwave on HIGH 2 minutes). Spoon into eggplant (aubergine) shells. Top with grated cheese and sprinkle with breadcrumbs. Toast under griller until golden brown.

Serve immediately as a main course or as a side dish with lamb or Cutlets en Croute.

SERVES 2

Ratatouille is a vegetable casserole originating in the Provence region of France.

VEGETABLES WITH AIOLI

- *250 g (8 oz) pumpkin, peeled*
- *2 zucchini (courgette), trimmed*
- *2 chokos, peeled*
- *1 carrot, scraped*
- *½ head cauliflower or broccoli*
- *4 button squash*

AIOLI

- *1 clove garlic, crushed*
- *2 egg yolks*
- *1 cup (250 ml/8 fl oz) virgin olive oil*

Cut vegetables into strips, break cauliflower or broccoli into florets. Boil or steam vegetables until just tender (or microwave on HIGH for 5 minutes).

To Prepare Aioli: Beat garlic and egg yolks together for 1 minute, continue to beat whilst gradually adding oil (this can be done in a blender or with a hand beater), continue beating until thick.

To Serve: Drizzle aioli over hot vegetables and serve with grills or roasts.

SERVES 6

SIX GROUPS OF OILS

- DELICATE AND AROMATIC: Sesame, pumpkin, grape, walnut oil. Must be refrigerated once opened.

- SATURATED OILS: Coconut, animal oils. These are strong oils and not recommended for cooking if on a low cholesterol diet.

- MONO-UNSATURATED: Peanut, olive. These oils break down at high temperature so should only be used for salads, dressings and quick and light frying eg sautéing.

- VIRGIN OLIVE OIL: Is made from the first pressing of the olive and hence is a fine, delicate oil most suitable for cold dishes and dressings.

- SOLIDIFIED OILS: These are processed to remain solid at room temperature eg copha, processed oils. They are often cheaper than oil and are ideal for deep frying.

- POLY-UNSATURATED: Sunflower, safflower, corn and soybean, not recommended for high temperature frying as the flavour deteriorates. Mainly used for dressings.

Crisp Fries

FRYING

There are three types of frying.

DRY FRYING: Where 1 tablespoon of oil is heated in a pan or food is fried in its own fat eg bacon rashers.

SHALLOW FRYING: Ideal for leftovers, use approximately 0.5 cm to 1 cm (¼ to ½ in) oil, heated in a pan.

DEEP FRYING: Using oil in a deep fryer to completely cover food.

CRISP FRIES

Pumpkin is best peeled, sliced in thin slices and half cooked by boiling, steaming or microwaving. Drain and pat dry before dipping into batter or covering with egg and breadcrumbs (see recipes below). Deep fry. Drain well before serving (flesh should be just tender as fully cooking may cause the slices to break).

Zucchini (courgette) should be sliced in thin slices. Place in a bowl, pour boiling water over zucchini (courgette) and stand for 2 minutes. Drain and pat dry before dipping in batter or coating with egg and breadcrumbs. Deep fry. Drain well before serving.

BATTER 1

125 g (4 oz) plain flour
1 egg, separated
pinch of salt
cold water, to mix

Sift flour into a mixing bowl. Stir egg yolk into flour, whisk egg white until stiff, fold into flour. Add salt and sufficient water to form a thick batter. Use immediately.

BATTER 2

125 g (4 oz) plain flour
beer, to mix

Place flour in a bowl, beat in beer until mixture forms a thick liquid. Use immediately.

BREADCRUMB COATING

1 egg
2 tablespoons water
brown breadcrumbs or cornflake crumbs

Whisk egg and water together. Dip vegetables into mixture then toss in breadcrumbs until coated. Refrigerate for 20 minutes before deep or shallow frying.

EGG AND WATER

Using water with the egg prevents the coating sticking to pan during frying.

BASKET OF SALAD

BASKET

1 loaf of white bread, unsliced

2 cloves garlic, crushed

¼ cup (60 ml/2 fl oz) oil

FILLING

2 zucchini (courgette) roasted (see Note)

1 green capsicum (pepper) roasted (see Note)

½ cup sun-dried tomatoes, with oil

8 slices prosciutto ham, shredded

Preheat oven to 180°C (350°F).

To Prepare Basket: With a sharp bread knife, remove end crusts from bread, cut four slices 10 cm (4 in) thick, remove crusts, carefully hollow out centre, leaving a base and sides.

Combine garlic and oil and brush over the baskets inside and out. Place on a baking tray and bake until golden, approximately 15 to 20 minutes.

To Prepare Filling: Thinly slice the sun-dried tomatoes, place in a bowl with 2 tablespoons of tomato oil, sliced roasted zucchini (courgette) and capsicum (pepper) and prosciutto. Mix to coat ingredients with oil. Pile into baskets.

Note: To roast vegetables, place whole vegetable in a moderate oven 180°C (350°F) for 20 minutes. Cool. Capsicum should be cut in half and seeds removed before roasting.

SERVES 6

PUMPKIN CROQUETTES

1 cup mashed pumpkin

1 cup cooked, finely chopped, meat, fish, (tinned or fresh), chicken or vegetables

1 egg

plain flour, to mix

egg and breadcrumb coating (see recipe page 52)

oil for deep frying

Combine pumpkin, cooked meat and egg. Add sufficient flour to make a firm mixture. Dip spoonfuls into breadcrumb coating, and shape into a 'cork shape'. Refrigerate for 20 minutes before deep frying.

MAKES 12 CROQUETTES

OILS

• Oil is a refined liquid made from extracts of seeds, nuts, fruits and animal fats and is liquid at normal temperatures.

• Oil is soluble in ether or alcohol but not in water.

• Cooking oils have been refined to be almost odourless and have a subtle flavour.

• Used and unused oils should never be mixed.

• Oils may be used several times, if they are strained and stored in an airtight container.

• If oil begins to 'smoke' it is a sign that the oil has begun to break down and should be discarded.

Basket of Salad

GINGER BAKED PUMPKIN

This recipe is based on a Caucasian dish.

- *1 butternut pumpkin, washed*
- *½ cup (125 ml/4 fl oz) water*
- *125 g (4 oz) sugar*
- *2.5 cm (1 in) piece fresh ginger, peeled and finely sliced*
- *juice of 1 lemon*
- *1 tablespoon almonds and 1 tablespoon pistachio nuts, dry fried until lightly brown, to garnish.*

Preheat oven to 180° C (350°F).

Slice pumpkin into 2.5 cm (1 in) slices. Remove seeds and membrane. Place in a baking dish. Combine water, sugar, ginger and juice in a saucepan and stir over heat until sugar dissolves. Bring to the boil and simmer for 3 minutes. Pour over pumpkin. Bake for 35 to 40 minutes until pumpkin is tender.

Serve garnished with nuts as an accompaniment to roasts or grills.

SERVES 6

WHOLE BAKED PUMPKIN

- *1 whole round pumpkin*
- *butter*
- *milk*
- *2 teaspoons seasoning (choose whichever you prefer: ground ginger, cinnamon, nutmeg, curry powder, salt and pepper)*

Preheat oven to 200°C (400°F).

Choose a small pumpkin, cut a slice from the top. Scoop out seeds, replace top. Place in a baking dish and bake for 1½ to 2 hours or until the inside is tender (remove top slice to test inside, replace top slice).

Carefully scoop out cooked flesh, place in a bowl mash well with butter, milk and seasoning of your choice. Return to shell bake for a further 10 minutes.

Serve as a centrepiece on a large platter with other vegetables or meats.

SERVES 4

PUMPKIN BAKE

This recipe can be cooked in your microwave.

- *500 g (1 lb) pumpkin, peeled, sliced approximately 0.5 cm (¼ in) thick*
- *2 teaspoons cornflour*
- *1 cup (250 ml/8 fl oz) milk*
- *125 g (4 oz) cheese, grated*
- *1 tablespoon chopped chives*

Preheat oven to 180°C (350°F).

Place pumpkin slices in a shallow greased baking dish.

Combine cornflour and milk in a pan, stirring until mixture boils (or microwave on HIGH for 2 minutes, then beat vigorously).

Pour sauce over pumpkin, top with cheese and sprinkle with chives.

Bake for 35 minutes or until pumpkin is tender, (or microwave on HIGH for 6 minutes).

Variation: Add 1 teaspoon French mustard to sauce.

SERVES 6

TO CRUSH GINGER

Place a cube of ginger in a garlic press, squeeze out the juice, discard the fibres.

CUCUMBER FLORENTINE

- *3 tablespoons olive oil*
- *2 cloves garlic, crushed*
- *freshly ground black pepper*
- *2 cucumbers, cut lengthwise, then into 5 cm (2 in) lengths*
- *½ cup (125 ml/4 fl oz) tomato purée*
- *fresh parsley, finely chopped*
- *1 teaspoon ground oregano*

Heat oil in a frying pan and add garlic and pepper. Fry cucumber pieces until the skins become bright green. Stir in remaining ingredients and simmer on low heat for 5 minutes (or to cook in microwave, combine all ingredients and cook on HIGH for 3 minutes).

Serve as a side dish with meat or as part of an antipasto.

SERVES 6

OVEN BAKED SQUASH

1 large squash
1 stalk celery, finely chopped
1 tomato, finely chopped
grated cheese

Preheat oven to 180°C (350°F).

Place a small amount of water in a cake tin. Cut end from squash so it will sit evenly in cake tin. Remove top and scoop out seeds and a little squash flesh. Fill with celery, tomato and cheese, replace top.

Bake for 40 to 45 minutes or until tender.

Serve with grills, fries or roasts.

Variation: Add a rasher of finely diced and fried bacon to the mixture.

SERVES 6

ROAST PUMPKIN

Roast pumpkin is the perfect accompaniment to roast meats.

pumpkin
oil

Preheat oven to 200°C (400°F).

Cut pumpkin into wedges no thicker than 1 cm (½ in). Peel and place in cold water for 15 minutes. Drain and pat dry. Place on wire rack over a baking dish and brush both sides lightly with oil. Cook for 30 minutes. Turn and cook for a further 15 minutes or until soft.

CUCUMBERS AND MUSHROOMS IN A CREAM SAUCE

3 cucumbers, peeled and sliced in half, lengthwise
pinch salt
1 tablespoon butter
8 mushrooms, sliced
1 cup (250 ml/8 fl oz) cream
1 teaspoon cornflour
1 tablespoon water
½ teaspoon chopped fresh tarragon

Place cucumbers with salt in a pan. Cover with water, bring to the boil then simmer for 5 minutes (or microwave cucumbers in a little water with salt added and cook on HIGH for 2 minutes). Drain.

Heat butter in a frying pan and lightly fry mushrooms, stirring for approximately 3 minutes. Stir in cream, coating the mushrooms, until simmering. Mix cornflour, water and tarragon together and stir into mushrooms. Stir until cream mixture thickens.

To Prepare in a Microwave: Combine sauce ingredients, stir well, cook on HIGH for 2 minutes, stir well.

Spoon sauce over the cucumbers. Serve with grills.

Variation: 1 bacon rasher can be chopped and fried and added to sauce or replace tarragon with thyme.

SERVES 6

BAKED ZUCCHINI (COURGETTE) WITH PESTO

6 zucchini (courgette) or 1 marrow

PESTO

1 bunch fresh basil
6 sprigs fresh parsley
1 tablespoon pine nuts
1 clove garlic, crushed
1 tablespoon virgin olive oil

TOPPING

freshly grated Parmesan cheese
extra olive oil

Preheat oven to 180°C (350°F).

Trim ends and split zucchini lengthwise. If using marrow, trim ends, cut in half lengthwise and remove seeds. Using a metal teaspoon make a channel or shell in the vegetable. Place in greased shallow ovenproof dish.

To Prepare Pesto: Combine ingredients and process until smooth. Spoon pesto into shells.

To Prepare Topping: Sprinkle shells with a little cheese and brush with extra olive oil.

Bake for 20 to 25 minutes, or until tender.

SERVES 6

TIMBALES

Timbales are similar to a custard and are cooked in a custard mould. They are served at room temperature, as an entrée or as a vegetable with a main course.

PEA AND PUMPKIN TIMBALES

> *4 eggs*
>
> *300 g (10 oz) thick sour cream*

PUMPKIN TIMBALE

> *300 g (10 oz) pumpkin, cooked and dry mashed*
>
> *½ teaspoon nutmeg*

PEA TIMBALE

> *500 g (16 oz) fresh or frozen peas, shelled and cooked*
>
> *1 tablespoon freshly grated Parmesan cheese*
>
> *3 sprigs fresh mint*

Preheat oven to 150°C (300°F).

Grease six ½ cup (125 ml/4 fl oz) dariole or custard moulds.

Beat eggs and cream together and divide into two bowls.

To Prepare Pumpkin: Place pumpkin and nutmeg in one bowl of egg mixture. Beat until smooth.

To Prepare Peas: Push peas through a sieve or process with cheese and add chopped mint. Add to egg mixture in second bowl. Stir to combine.

Half fill the dariole or custard moulds with pumpkin mixture and top with pea mixture.

Place moulds in a baking dish of water. Cover with greased aluminium foil. Bake until set, approximately 30 minutes. Remove from oven, allow moulds to stand in the water for 3 to 5 minutes, remove aluminium foil. Carefully run a knife between mould and timbale to loosen. Place dinner plate on top of timbale, turn plate over, carefully lift mould away.

Serve with roast veal or rack of lamb.

Variation: Can be served with a tomato coulis or chive hollandaise (see recipes below and overleaf).

SERVES 6

TOMATO COULIS

> *1 tablespoon oil*
>
> *1 onion, finely chopped*
>
> *1 clove garlic, crushed*
>
> *400 g (12½ oz) can tomatoes*
>
> *pinch of sugar*

Heat oil in a frying pan and fry onion and garlic until transparent. Add tomatoes (with their liquid) and sugar. Bring to the boil. Process in a food processor or push through a sieve. Serve as a sauce around Pea and Pumpkin Timbale.

Pea and Pumpkin Timbales served with Tomato Coulis (recipe above), Spring Salad (page 59)

CHIVE HOLLANDAISE

¼ cup (60 ml/2 fl oz) white
   vinegar

2 egg yolks

juice of ½ lemon

2 tablespoons chopped chives

125 g (4 oz) butter

Boil vinegar in a ceramic lined or stainless steel pan until reduced by half. Remove from heat, beat in egg yolks, lemon juice and chives. Continue beating until smooth. Heat butter until it has melted then quickly whisk into the egg yolk mixture.

Serve as a sauce poured around Pea and Pumpkin Timbales.

Variation: Spoon a little Tomato Coulis around half the timbale and a little Chive Hollandaise around the other side (see Pea and Pumpkin Timbales, page 57).

PUMPKIN SEED OIL

Pumpkin seed oil is predominantly unsaturated. It can be pale yellow to dark brown in colour, bland to aromatic in flavour depending on the processing method. Seeds contain 30% to 40% oil. Only a few countries, including Yugoslavia, produce the oil for cooking.

MOSAIC OF VEGETABLES

This dish is ideal for a buffet.

SAUCE

3 spring onions, trimmed and
   diced

4 stalks fennel leaves or dill,
   chopped

1 teaspoon dried rosemary

1 tablespoon oil

2 tablespoons brown
   or wine vinegar

freshly ground black pepper

1 tablespoon brown sugar

2 tablespoons water

VEGETABLES

1 small butternut pumpkin,
   peeled and seeded

4 zucchini (courgette), chokos
   or marrow, peeled

3 red capsicums (peppers)

12 mushrooms, stalks removed

20 g (½ oz) butter

4 firm tomatoes

1 teaspoon ground thyme

plain flour

1 egg and 1 tablespoon water,
   combined

breadcrumbs

oil for shallow frying

1 tablespoon oil extra, to serve

2 teaspoons dried or fresh
   rosemary, fennel or dill sprigs,
   to garnish

Preheat oven to 180°C (350°F).

To Prepare Sauce. Place all ingredients in a saucepan. Bring to simmering point, cook until onions are tender, stirring occasionally to prevent sticking. Spread in the base of a shallow greased ovenproof dish.

To Prepare Vegetables: Pumpkin: Cut pumpkin into six slices 1 cm (½ in) thick, then cut those slices in half to make 12 slices. Steam or boil, (or microwave on HIGH for 2 minutes) until almost tender but still firm, drain carefully.

Zucchini (courgette) or choko or marrow: Trim ends, slice 1 cm (½ in) thick. Boil or steam (or microwave on HIGH for 2 minutes), until tender but still holding their shape, drain.

Capsicum (peppers): Seed and cut into 12 thick slices. Steam or boil (or microwave on HIGH for 2 minutes), drain.

Mushroom: Melt butter in a pan, sauté mushrooms until tender, turning once (or microwave, with butter on HIGH for 2 minutes), drain.

Tomatoes: Remove ends, slice each tomato into 3, sprinkle with thyme. Coat both sides with flour, toss in egg and breadcrumbs. Shallow fry until brown, turning once, drain.

To Assemble: Divide vegetables into 3 lots. Arrange on top of the sauce overlapping each row on the row below. Repeat 3 times, making 15 rows of vegetables: 1st row pumpkin slices, 2nd row mushrooms, 3rd row capsicum, 4th row tomatoes, 5th row zucchini or marrow.

Cover with greased aluminium foil, and bake for 10 minutes.

To serve: Brush with extra oil, sprinkle with extra rosemary, garnish with dill or fennel sprigs.

The salad platter is a canvas of shapes and colours. Served all year round either as an entrée, between courses or as a complement to a main dish.

WINTER SALAD

½ head broccoli

½ head cauliflower

3 carrots, scraped, cut into thin sticks and then cut in half again

6 yellow squash, cut in half

3 spring onions or shallots

1 red capsicum (pepper) seeded and cut into thin strips

DRESSING

2 tablespoons French mustard

2 tablespoons seeded mustard

6 tablespoons cream cheese

light sour cream, to taste

Break broccoli and cauliflower into florets and plunge into a pot of boiling water for 3 minutes. Remove with a slotted spoon, refresh under cold running water. Repeat with carrots and squash.

Slice white part of onion or shallot into thin slices and dice green shoots.

To Prepare Dressing: Combine all ingredients in a bowl except sour cream. Place bowl in hot water (or microwave on HIGH for 30 seconds only), just to soften the mixture. Add a little sour cream to make into a thick liquid consistency.

To Serve: Place all prepared vegetables in a pottery bowl, toss with dressing just before serving.

Variation: Add 12 crisp croutons (see soup accompaniments page 19), or add 6 mushrooms cut into slices and lightly fried in butter, or substitute blue-vein cheese for cream cheese.

SERVES 6

Place dressing ingredients in a screw top jar, cover and shake well to mix.

SPRING SALAD

250 g (8 oz) pumpkin, peeled, seeded, diced and cooked

12 stalks fresh asparagus, cut into 3.5 cm (1½ in) pieces and steamed

3 green zucchini (courgettes) ends trimmed, cut into thin rounds and blanched in hot water

2 potatoes, peeled, cooked and diced into same sized pieces as pumpkin

425 g (13½ oz) can baby corn, drained

6 yellow tear drop tomatoes, cut in half

6 red cherry tomatoes cut in half

DRESSING

6 leaves fresh basil

6 leaves fresh mint

3 fresh parsley sprigs, stems removed

sprig fresh rosemary or thyme

½ cup commercial Italian dressing

juice ½ lemon

nasturtium flowers, washed, to garnish (optional)

Prepare vegetables as directed.

To Prepare Dressing: Pound or finely chop herbs, add to Italian dressing with lemon juice, mix well. Allow to stand for 2 hours before use. Re-mix before pouring.

To serve: Combine all vegetables in a serving bowl, serve dressing in a jug and garnish salad with nasturtium flowers if desired (these are edible).

SERVES 6

SUMMER SALAD

1 iceberg or butterhead lettuce

1 zucchini (courgette) trimmed, finely sliced lengthwise

1 Lebanese cucumber, thinly sliced

12 cherry tomatoes

3 hard-boiled eggs, shelled and cut into quarters

6 cos lettuce leaves, shredded

1 avocado, peeled and sliced

DRESSING

6 anchovy fillets, stuffed with capers

2 egg yolks

3 teaspoons French mustard

¼ teaspoon Tabasco sauce

1 teaspoon Worcestershire sauce

¾ cup (185 ml/6 fl oz) virgin olive oil

3 tablespoons wine vinegar

juice of 1 lemon

Break lettuce into six large lettuce cups and place in iced water for 5 to 10 minutes. Remove and shake dry. Place on a platter or bowl or on six individual plates. Divide remaining vegetables and eggs into the lettuce cups.

To Prepare Dressing: Combine all ingredients in a blender and process until smooth, pour into a jug.

Serve lettuce cups with a jug of dressing.

Variation: Add 24 croutons, (see soup accompaniments page 19) and 2 rashers bacon, finely shredded and fried until crisp.

SERVES 6

PUMPKIN SEED AND CHICKEN SALAD

300 g (10 oz) cooked chicken, sliced

1 small can mandarin segments, drained or 1 fresh mandarin peeled, separated and seeded

3 stalks celery, diced

Dressing

½ cup (125 ml/4 fl oz) mayonnaise

½ cup (125 ml/4 fl oz) thickened cream

leaves of rocket (or lettuce), to garnish

2 tablespoons roasted pumpkin seeds, to garnish (see Note)

Combine chicken, mandarin segments, and celery in a bowl.

To Prepare Dressing: Mix together mayonnaise and cream.

Pour dressing over chicken. Mix together gently, cover and chill.

To Serve: Place rocket or lettuce leaves on a serving plate, spoon on chicken mixture and top with roasted pumpkin seeds.

Note: To roast pumpkin seeds, place seeds in a heavy based pan and stir over heat for 1 minute.

SERVES 6

TAHINI

Tahini is a white, slightly bitter paste, made from raw sesame seeds, oil and flavourings.

MOULDED NUT SALAD

2 cucumbers, finely sliced

125 g (4 oz) ricotta cheese

250 g (8 oz) pumpkin, cooked and dry mashed

3 tablespoons tahini

125 g (4 oz) raw cashew nuts, broken into small pieces

1 Spanish onion, peeled and finely diced

tomatoes, thinly sliced, to garnish

Rinse a round bowl (approximately 16 cm x 8 cm (6½ in x 3 in)) with water. Drain, leaving beads of water inside the bowl. Line base and sides of bowl with cucumber slices, overlapping generously. Combine other ingredients press mixture together, place in bowl and press into cucumber lining. Chill for 1 hour.

To Serve: Place serving plate on top of bowl, turn over, carefully lift bowl leaving cucumber lined mould in centre of plate. Overlap tomato slices around base of salad mould.

SERVES 6

SALAD OF MARROW FLOWERS

12 small marrows with flowers attached or 12 zucchinis (courgettes) with flowers

1 tablespoon olive oil

1 Spanish onion, thinly sliced

½ cup fresh marjoram, chopped

juice of 1 lemon

freshly ground black pepper

12 black olives, pitted

red cabbage leaves, washed

400 g (12½ oz) sliced smoked chicken or salmon

Cook marrows or zucchini with flowers in boiling water, until just tender. (You can also microwave on HIGH for 2 minutes, test cook a further minute if not tender). Drain carefully. Heat oil in a frying pan and fry onion until transparent. Add marjoram, lemon juice, pepper and olives. Arrange washed cabbage leaves on a platter, place onion mixture in centre of leaves. Arrange slices smoked chicken or salmon on top of onion mixture and place marrow or zucchini with flowers across the top of the chicken or salmon. Chill thoroughly before serving.

SERVES 6

MARJORAM

Marjoram was a sign of happiness in ancient Greece.

Pictured on previous pages: Pumpkin Seed and Chicken Salad (recipe above), Marrow Purée with Herbs (page 47) (a great accompaniment to grilled meats)

THAI NOODLE SALAD

500 g (16 oz) vermicelli pasta, cooked in boiling water until tender

2 carrots, scraped and cut into julienne sticks

2 zucchini (courgette) trimmed and cut into julienne strips

150 g (5 oz) freshly cooked prawns (shrimps), shelled and deveined

DRESSING

½ cup (125 ml/4 fl oz) oil

juice of 1 lime

2 tablespoons dark soy sauce

1 tablespoon brown sugar

2 tablespoons fish sauce

½ cup fresh basil, chopped

½ cup fresh spearmint, chopped

½ cup fresh coriander, chopped

Combine pasta, carrots, zucchini (courgette) and prawns (shrimps) in a serving bowl.

To Prepare Dressing: Mix all dressing ingredients together, until sugar dissolves.

To Serve: Toss salad with dressing and serve at room temperature.

SERVES 6

CUCUMBER SALAD

2 cucumbers

salt

250 g (8 oz) natural yoghurt or thick sour cream

1 cup (250 ml/8 fl oz) mayonnaise

2 shallots (spring onions), finely chopped

60 g (2 oz) walnuts, chopped

60 g (2 oz) sultanas

8 sprigs fresh mint, chopped

pinch of dried basil

Slice cucumbers thinly, place in a colander, sprinkle with salt, allow to stand for 20 minutes. Drain.

Combine cucumber with all remaining ingredients.

Serve well chilled.

SERVES 4 TO 6

ZUCCHINI (COURGETTE) SALAD

500 g (16 oz) zucchini (courgette)

virgin olive oil

3 cloves garlic, cut into slivers

20 fresh mint leaves, chopped

juice of ½ lemon

2 tablespoons wine vinegar

½ tablespoon finely chopped red chillies

Slice zucchini (courgettes) lengthwise into 0.5 cm (¼ in) thick slices. Brush with oil, place on a griller tray, grill until lightly brown. Carefully turn over and grill other side.

Place in a serving bowl. Combine remaining ingredients, pour over zucchini (courgettes). Allow to stand for 1 hour or overnight before serving.

SERVES 6

Baking and Desserts

Pumpkin and squash for dessert might sound a little unusual, but only until you've tried these wonderful recipes. This chapter reveals the secrets of Pumpkin Pie and shows you some delicious new desserts.

NOTES

- 500 g (16 oz) wedge, of uncooked pumpkin, yields 1 cup cooked and mashed pumpkin.

- Butternut, jarrahdale and jap pumpkins are most suitable for pies, desserts and cakes.

- Margarine may be substituted for butter in all recipes.

- Wholemeal plain flour may be substituted for plain flour.

- Use a sheet of greaseproof paper to roll pastry out, once used, it can then be discarded with the scraps wrapped inside.

- Pumpkin pies do not set firmly, they will be soft when cooked.

- Trim edges of pastry with back of knife blade. Pinch pastry edge with thumb and forefinger to form a patterned rim on the pastry case.

PUMPKIN QUICHE

*1 uncooked pastry case
(see recipes page 67)*

125 g (4 oz) tasty cheese, grated

30 g (1 oz) butter

6 shallots (spring onions), finely chopped

½ teaspoon nutmeg

½ teaspoon freshly ground pepper

½ teaspoon ground ginger

3 eggs, separated

¾ cup (185 ml/6 fl oz) cream or milk

1 cup cooked pumpkin, mashed

Preheat oven to 190°C (375°F).

Make pastry case as directed.

Sprinkle grated cheese over pastry base. Melt butter in a frying pan and lightly fry shallots (spring onions) for 2 minutes. Add spices, egg yolks, cream or milk and pumpkin. Whisk egg whites until stiff, fold into mixture. Hold a spoon upside down in base of pastry case, then pour filling mixture into case, remove spoon. Holding a spoon in the base prevents the action of pouring weakening the pastry base.

Bake in oven for 10 minutes, then lower heat to 180°C (350°F) and bake for a further 30 minutes.

Serve cut into slices whilst still hot, with a salad.

Variation: Add 2 rashers bacon, rind and fat removed, diced.

SERVES 4 TO 6

IT'S AS EASY AS PIE!

The expression 'easy as pie' is an American term dating from the early 20th century referring to the eating of, rather than the preparation of the pie.

PUMPKIN BRAN PIE

*1 uncooked pastry case
(see recipes page 67)*

*2 tablespoons oil
or 40 g (1½ oz) butter*

500 g (16 oz) pumpkin, peeled and grated

4 medium potatoes, peeled and grated

1 onion, grated

3 stalks celery, finely chopped

2 eggs

½ cup (125 ml/4 fl oz) milk

½ teaspoon ground nutmeg

TOPPING

60 g (2 oz) plain flour

1 tablespoon bran

1 tablespoon butter

125 g (4 oz) grated cheese

Preheat oven to 180°C (350°F).

Make pastry case as directed.

Heat oil or butter in a frying pan and gently stir-fry vegetables until potato is just soft but not mushy. Beat eggs, milk and nutmeg together. Add vegetables. Spoon into the pastry case.

To Prepare Topping: Combine flour and bran, rub butter into mixture with tips of fingers until crumbly. Mix in cheese. Sprinkle over vegetable filling. Cover with greased aluminium foil. Bake for 1 hour. Remove aluminium foil, continue baking until topping browns slightly.

Variations: Substitute rice bran for bran, or 1 small can tuna may be added to filling, or 1 cup cottage cheese may be added to filling.

SERVES 6

Pictured on previous pages: American Pumpkin Pie (page 70), Zucchini (Courgette), Apple and Walnut Cake (page 75), Savoury Zucchini (Courgette) Scones (page 79)

Pastries

BASIC SHORT CRUST PASTRY

125 g (4 oz) plain flour

pinch salt

90 g (3 oz) butter, cubed (use salted butter in pastry for savoury pies and unsalted butter for sweet pies)

1 egg yolk

squeeze of lemon juice

cold water, to mix

Sift flour and salt into a bowl. With the fingertips, rub in butter until mixture resembles fine breadcrumbs. Make a hollow in the centre. With a knife, cut in egg yolk and lemon juice, then cut in 1 tablespoon water, stir, adding more water if necessary to form a stiff dough.

Sprinkle a sheet of greaseproof paper with extra flour, turn out dough. Knead lightly until a smooth ball forms.

Dust rolling pin with flour and roll dough to fit the size of the dish. Place rolling pin in centre of pastry lift one end of the paper and flip the pastry onto the rolling pin, then lift rolling pin with pastry across a 20 cm (8 in) pie dish. Remove rolling pin, and gently push pastry into dish. Trim edges. Chill until ready to use.

To Make Sweet Pastry: Add 2 tablespoons icing sugar or caster sugar to the flour in the basic recipe.

MAKES SUFFICIENT FOR THE BASE OF A 20 CM (8 IN) PIE DISH

GLUTEN-FREE PASTRY

370 g (12 oz) brown rice flour

½ teaspoon baking powder

150 g (5 oz) butter, cubed

cold water, to mix

Sift brown rice flour and baking powder together. Rub in butter with tips of fingers until mixture resembles fine breadcrumbs. With a knife, cut in sufficient cold water to make a stiff dough. Turn out onto a lightly floured sheet of greaseproof paper.

Knead gently until mixture forms a smooth ball.

Dust rolling pin with extra brown rice flour, roll out pastry to fit a 20 cm (8 in) greased pie plate. Trim edges. Chill until ready to use.

Note: This pastry tends to be crumbly. If pastry breaks while lifting it into the dish, place pastry into centre of dish then mould pastry with fingertips to line the pie dish.

MAKES SUFFICIENT FOR THE BASE OF A 20 CM (8 IN) PIE DISH

BISCUIT (COOKIE) PASTRY

18 ginger or honey snap biscuits (cookies)

2 tablespoons unsalted butter, melted

Preheat oven to 180°C (350°F).

Crush biscuits finely. Transfer to a bowl and stir in butter. Pat into a greased 20 cm (8 in) pie dish. Bake for 10 minutes. Cool.

MAKES SUFFICIENT FOR THE BASE OF A 20 CM (8 IN) PIE DISH

KNEADING

The dough is folded and pushed down with the palm of the hand, then the process is repeated gently, only until the dough forms a light, smooth ball.

TO CRUSH BISCUITS

Place biscuits in a plastic bag and crush finely with a rolling pin, or crush in a food processor.

TO SAVE TIME

Make double quantity of pastry and freeze until required.

ZUCCHINI (COURGETTE) QUICHE

1 uncooked pastry case
  (see recipes page 67)

1 teaspoon butter

3 zucchini (courgette) trimmed,
  and finely sliced

125 g (4 oz) tasty cheese, grated

125 g (4 oz) cottage cheese

3 tablespoons chopped fresh
  parsley

6 fresh basil leaves, chopped

¾ cup (185 ml/6 fl oz) milk

3 eggs, separated

Preheat oven to 190°C (375°F).

Make pastry case as directed. Melt butter in a frying pan and lightly fry zucchini (courgette). Place zucchini (courgette) in base of pastry case. Combine cheeses, herbs, milk and egg yolks in a bowl, mix well. Whisk egg whites stiffly, fold into cheese mixture. Hold a spoon upside down in the base of the pastry case. Pour cheese mixture over zucchini (courgette), remove spoon.

Bake in the oven for 10 minutes then reduce temperature to 180°C (350°F) and cook for a further 30 minutes.

Serve hot, cut into slices, with a tomato salad.

Note: Zucchini (courgette), has a crisp texture when quiche is cooked, if a softer texture is preferred, sauté zucchini (courgette), until soft, then place in pastry case.

SERVES 6

Zucchini (Courgette) Quiche (recipe above), Pumpkin Syrup Cake (page 72), Pumpkin Muffins (page 79)

CHEESE AND NUT PIE WITH LIQUEUR CREAM

1 biscuit pie crust, cooked
(see recipe page 67)

250 g (8 oz) soft cream cheese

125 g (4 oz) sugar

1 cup cooked pumpkin

2 eggs, separated

½ teaspoon ground cloves

1 tablespoon honey

½ cup (125 ml/4 fl oz) thick
cream

almond halves or crushed
macadamia nuts

LIQUEUR CREAM

300 ml (10 fl oz) cream

1 tablespoon icing sugar

1 tablespoon Grand Marnier
or Cointreau liqueur

Preheat oven to 180°C (350°F).

Prepare biscuit crust as directed.
Beat cream cheese and sugar
together. Add pumpkin, egg yolks,
cloves, honey and cream. Whisk egg
whites until stiff, fold into mixture.
Spoon into crust, cover and top with
almond halves or crushed macadamia
nuts. Bake for 1 hour, test. Allow to
cool at room temperature.

Cheese and Nut Pie With Liqueur Cream

To Prepare Liqueur Cream: Whip
cream with icing sugar and liqueur
of your choice until thick.

Serve with Liqueur Cream.

SERVES 6

TO SOFTEN HONEY

To melt honey, place jar in microwave
oven on a low setting, without
lid, for 30 seconds.

PUMPKIN POTS WITH ORANGE GLAZE

This recipe should be made 24 hours before serving.

1 orange

GLAZE

185 g (6 oz) sugar

¾ cup (185 ml/6 fl oz) water

CUSTARD

1 cup cooked pumpkin

1½ cups (375 ml/12 fl oz) milk

2 eggs, beaten

2 tablespoons brown sugar

1 teaspoon ground cinnamon

Preheat oven to 150°C (300°F).

Grease six small ramekins or dariole moulds and place in a baking dish with 5 cm (2 in) of water. Grate orange rind, without any pith and squeeze orange for juice.

To Prepare Glaze: Place sugar and water in a pan. Stir over heat until sugar dissolves, do not continue to stir. Allow glaze to bubble until it is a light brown colour. Carefully and slowly add orange juice (as it tends to splutter). Pour glaze equally into prepared moulds.

To Prepare Custard: Combine, pumpkin, milk, eggs, sugar, cinnamon and orange rind. Spoon over glaze in base of moulds. Cover with greased aluminium foil (for oven) or plastic wrap (for microwave). Bake in the dish of water for 30 to 40 minutes, until set (or microwave in dish of water on MEDIUM for 10 minutes, test with a knife blade, if required, cook at 2 minute intervals until set).

Refrigerate for 24 hours. Turn out onto individual dessert plates with glaze on top (glaze should run over custard when turned out).

Serve well chilled with whipped cream, garnished with candied orange strips. (See toppings in cake making page 74.)

SERVES 6

DARIOLE CUPS

Darioles are small, cylindrical, metal moulds suitable for constant, high heat.

AMERICAN PUMPKIN PIE

1 uncooked pastry case, plain or sweet (see recipe page 67)

1½ cups cooked pumpkin

1 cup (250 ml/8 fl oz) milk

2 eggs

60 g (2 oz) brown sugar

1 teaspoon ground cinnamon

½ teaspoon ground ginger

½ teaspoon ground nutmeg

Preheat oven to 200°C (400°F).

Make pastry case as directed.

Combine all filling ingredients. Beat well until light. Spoon into pastry case. Bake for 40 to 45 minutes Test by sliding a knife blade into centre of pie, if cooked, the blade will come out clean, however, this filling does have a soft texture.

Serve cold, with ice cream, or just prior to serving, spread top with whipped cream sprinkled with chopped walnuts, or whipped cream with 1 teaspoon of ground ginger and 1 teaspoon sugar. Alternatively, cut pie into wedges, place on serving plates, cover with whipped cream. Make a hollow in cream, fill with a pool of honey.

SERVES 6

THANKSGIVING

Pumpkin pie is traditionally served on American Thanksgiving day.

PUMPKIN CHIFFON PIE

1 biscuit pie crust, cooked (see recipe page 67)

1 tablespoon gelatine

¼ cup (60 ml/2 fl oz) hot water

185 g (6 oz) brown sugar

2 teaspoons cinnamon

½ teaspoon ground nutmeg

1 cup cooked pumpkin

3 eggs, separated

½ cup (125 ml/4 fl oz) milk

3 tablespoons caster sugar

Preheat oven to 180°C (350°F).

Prepare biscuit crust as directed.

Stir gelatine and water together, set aside. Combine sugar, spices, pumpkin, egg yolks and milk in a pan. Beat well, bring to the boil, stirring all the time and allow to boil for 1 minute. Stir in gelatine mixture. Cool.

Whisk egg whites until stiff, gradually add sugar, a little at a time, whisk until glossy.

Beat pumpkin mixture until smooth, fold in egg white mixture. Pile into pie crust. Chill for 2 hours.

Serve with ice cream or cream.

SERVES 6

SPARKLING FRUIT PUMPKIN PIE

1 uncooked pastry case, plain or sweet (see recipe page 67)

1 orange

1 cup cooked pumpkin, mashed

90 g (3 oz) sultanas

½ cup (125 ml/4 fl oz) evaporated milk or light cream

2 egg yolks

60 g (2 oz) brown sugar

TOPPING

2 egg whites

60 g (2 oz) caster sugar

extra sugar, to garnish

Preheat oven to 180°C (350°F).

Make pastry case as directed.

Cut orange in half and juice it, then finely grate the orange rind without any pith. Add rind and juice to other filling ingredients, mix well. Spoon into pastry case. Bake for 30 minutes, or until set. Remove from oven.

To Prepare Topping: Increase the oven temperature to 200°C (400°F). Whisk egg whites until very stiff, gradually add sugar, 1 teaspoon at a time, whisking well until all sugar is dissolved. Spoon over pie, making peaks of meringue. Bake until meringue is just lightly browned (approximately 7 minutes). This is a soft dessert meringue.

To Prepare Garnish: Sprinkle a little sugar over meringue to make it sparkle.

Serve immediately with a scoop of ice cream or custard.

SERVES 6

PUMPKIN CUSTARDS

Pumpkins were once used as containers to bake custards. The tops were cut off, the seeds removed and the shells filled with milk. They were then set by the open hearth to slowly cook.

STEAMED PUMPKIN PUDDING WITH APPLE CARAMEL

CARAMEL

30 g (1 oz) unsalted butter

60 g (2 oz) brown sugar

1 tablespoon honey (optional)

2 green apples

6 glacé cherries

CAKE

125 g (4 oz) butter

125 g (4 oz) brown sugar

2 eggs, beaten

1 cup cooked pumpkin

90 g (3 oz) self-raising flour

To Prepare Caramel: Beat butter, brown sugar and honey together. Spoon equal amounts of caramel into the base of six greased, small ramekins or dariole cups. Slice top and bottom from apples, peel and core. Slice each apple into 3 rounds. Place 1 round on top of caramel in each mould, place a glacé cherry in centre of each round of apple.

To Prepare Cake: Beat butter and sugar together until creamy. Beat in eggs then add pumpkin. Sift flour and stir into mixture. Spoon equal amounts of cake mixture carefully on top of apple.

Cover dariole moulds with greased aluminium foil and then the lid. Place moulds into a water-filled steamer. Steam 30 to 40 minutes.

To Prepare in Microwave: Cover moulds with plastic wrap. Cook on MEDIUM for 5 minutes. Test. If necessary cook at 1 minute intervals until cooked.

Test with a thin knife blade. The cake should be firm.

To Serve: Remove moulds from steamer. Place a serving plate on top of each mould, invert, so the apple and caramel is on top. Serve hot with ice cream or custard.

Note: Uncooked mixture can be frozen. Cook whilst still frozen.

Variation: Substitute gluten-free flour plus 1 teaspoon of baking powder for the self-raising flour.

SERVES 6

BETTER PASTRY

Pastry is lighter and crisper if it is refrigerated or frozen for a short while before baking.

SWEET PIES

To make a sweet pastry for a pie, add 2 tablespoons icing sugar or caster sugar, with flour in the basic recipe.

PECAN PIE

1 uncooked pastry case, plain or sweet (see recipe page 67)

2 eggs, beaten

200 g (6½ oz) carton natural yoghurt

1 teaspoon mixed spice

1 cup cooked pumpkin, mashed

90 g (3 oz) honey

TOPPING

250 g (8 oz) sugar

1 cup (250 ml/8 fl oz) water

1 teaspoon butter

60 g (2 oz) pecan nuts, shelled

Preheat oven to 180°C (350°F).

Make pastry case as directed.

Combine all filling ingredients. Spoon into pastry case. Bake for 30 to 40 minutes (test with knife blade) until set. Pour cooked topping over. Chill for at least 2 hours before serving.

To Prepare Topping: Place sugar and water in a pan, stir over heat until sugar dissolves. Bring to boil, do not stir once mixture begins to boil. Allow to boil rapidly until just turning light yellow. Remove immediately from heat. Add butter and nuts. Shake pan carefully until all nuts are covered with syrup. Pour over top of pie.

Note: If the syrup is allowed to become golden or brown in colour and more a toffee consistency it is a little difficult to cut through the topping, however it is still delicious, so do not discard.

SERVES 6

PUMPKIN SYRUP CAKE

Pictured on page 68.

half an orange

250 g (8 oz) butter

2 teaspoons ground ginger

½ teaspoon ground cinnamon

250 g (8 oz) sugar

3 eggs, separated

1 cup cooked, mashed pumpkin

125 g (4 oz) self-raising flour

125 g (4 oz) plain flour

1 teaspoon bicarbonate of soda

SYRUP

2 tablespoons orange juice

½ teaspoon ground ginger

250 g (8 oz) sugar

Note: This recipe can be halved to make one cake. Otherwise make the full recipe and freeze one half (cooked or uncooked) until required.

Preheat oven to 150°C (300°F).

Grate rind from half an orange without pith. Add rind to butter with ginger, cinnamon and sugar.

Pecan Pie (recipe above) served with Spicy Ice Cream (page 83)

COCONUT PIE

1 uncooked pastry case, plain or sweet (see recipe page 67)

2 eggs

60 g (2 oz) brown sugar

1 teaspoon ground cinnamon

½ teaspoon ground ginger

1 tablespoon golden syrup (corn syrup or treacle)

½ cup (125 ml/4 fl oz) milk

1 cup cooked pumpkin, mashed

30 g (1 oz) desiccated coconut

shredded coconut, lightly toasted, to decorate (see Note)

Note: To toast coconut, either place in a pan and stir over heat or toast in the oven, until lightly brown.

Preheat oven to 180°C (350°F).

Make pastry case as directed.

Beat eggs. Add all remaining ingredients and mix well. Spoon into pastry shell. Bake for 30 minutes.

To serve: Cover top with toasted coconut.

SERVES 6

Coconut Pie

Beat until white and fluffy. Beat in egg yolks, stir in pumpkin. Sift flours and bicarbonate of soda together, fold into mixture. Whisk egg whites until stiff, fold into mixture. Spoon into two greased (but not lined) 18 cm (7 in) cake tins. Bake for 1 hour. Test with a fine skewer. Remove from oven and leave cakes in tins.

To Prepare Syrup: Combine all ingredients in a pan, stir over heat until sugar dissolves. Bring to boil, simmer without stirring for 2 minutes. Remove from heat, allow bubbles to settle.

Pour syrup evenly over both cakes in tins. Allow to stand 15 minutes before turning out.

SUFFICIENT FOR TWO 18 CM (7 IN) SANDWICH CAKE TINS

NOTES

- Oven temperatures given in the following recipes are for fan forced ovens.

- For conventional ovens, increase temperatures 15°C to 20°C (60°F to 70°F).

- 500 g (16 oz) wedge uncooked pumpkin yields 1 cup cooked mashed pumpkin.

- 1 zucchini (courgette) weighs approximately 125 g (4 oz).

- Margarine may be substituted for butter in all recipes.

- Grease cake pan with a little butter on a piece of greaseproof paper or melt butter and use a brush to grease, then cut a piece of greaseproof paper to fit base and grease paper well.

- Always pre-heat the oven before baking cakes, scones, bread etc.

- Test by inserting a thin straw or fine skewer into centre of cake, if cooked, it will come out clean.

- All of the following cakes can be sliced warm and served with custard, ice cream or whipped cream as a dessert.

CINNAMON SUGAR

Brush cake with a little melted butter. Combine equal amounts of sugar and ground cinnamon. Sprinkle over warm cake.

BASIC ICING

155 g (5 oz) icing sugar

1 teaspoon unsalted butter

½ teaspoon vanilla flavouring essence

hot water, to mix

Sift icing sugar into a mixing bowl, beat in butter and vanilla and sufficient hot water to form a thick paste. Pour onto cake, allow icing to flow, then spread with a warmed flat knife. If you microwave the mixture on HIGH for 30 seconds before spreading, it helps the icing to flow easily and to set quickly.

Variations: There are numerous ways to vary icing. For each of the following variations add the extra ingredients to the basic recipe and mix well.

ORANGE ICING

1 tablespoon orange juice

grated rind of half an orange

COCONUT ICING

2 tablespoons desiccated coconut

CHOCOLATE ICING

1 tablespoon sifted cocoa

CHEESE ICING

250 g (8 oz) ricotta or cream cheese

1 tablespoon icing sugar, sifted

1 teaspoon grated lemon rind

CANDIED ORANGE PEEL

1 orange

2 tablespoons sugar

2 tablespoons water

Finely cut peel from orange. Ensure that there is no white pith remaining on the peel as this can give the peel a very bitter taste. Slice into long thin julienne strips. Combine sugar

and water in a pan, stir until sugar dissolves. Bring to boil. Allow to simmer until syrup has a glazed appearance (approximately 5 minutes), do not brown. Remove from heat and add orange peel, swirl to cover peel then drain on a paper towel. Cool and use to decorate cake.

CAUSES OF POOR RESULTS IN CAKE MAKING

COARSE TEXTURE
- too much raising agent
- insufficient creaming of sugar and butter
- too much flour
- mixture beaten too much once flour was added

FALLEN, SUNKEN
- too much sugar
- temperature too low
- insufficient baking time

CRACKED, RAISED CENTRE
- too stiff a mixture
- oven temperature too high
- cake pan too deep

STICKY ON TOP
- too much sugar
- sugar not sufficiently beaten or creamed

TUNNELS OR HOLES
- over-beating once liquid was added
- air trapped in cake mixture when spooning into pan.

CHOCOLATE ZUCCHINI (COURGETTE) CAKE

90 g (3 oz) cooking chocolate, broken into pieces

¼ cup (60 ml/2 fl oz) milk

90 g (3 oz) butter

1 teaspoon grated orange rind (without pith)

250 g (8 oz) sugar

2 eggs

155 g (5 oz) self-raising flour

1 cup finely grated zucchini (courgette)

1 tablespoon desiccated coconut

TOPPING

30 g (1 oz) plain flour

2 tablespoons brown sugar

20 g (½ oz) butter, softened

60 g (2 oz) walnuts, chopped

CREAM CHEESE FILLING

60 g (2 oz) cream cheese

20 g (½ oz) softened butter

2 tablespoons orange juice

40 g (1½ oz) icing sugar

Note: This cake is best eaten within two days of cooking. The amounts can be halved to make one cake. Otherwise make the full recipe and freeze one half (cooked or uncooked) until required.

Preheat oven to 180°C (350°F).

Grease two 18 cm (7 in) cake tins and line with greased paper in one piece. On one tin, bring the greased paper 5 cm (2 in) above the tin so that it forms a collar.

Heat milk and chocolate pieces together over a low heat, stirring until chocolate melts (or microwave on HIGH for 1 minute then stir until the chocolate melts).

Cream butter, orange rind and sugar together until fluffy and white. Beat in eggs. Add flour alternately with chocolate mixture and stir. Stir in zucchini (courgette) and coconut. Divide mixture evenly between the tins. Place topping on the cake which has the paper collar.

Bake for 25 to 30 minutes. Test with a fine skewer. Cool in the tin for 3 minutes.

Turn the plain cake out onto a wire cake cooling rack. Carefully hold the protuding paper of the topped cake with both hands and lift the cake from the tin. Place one hand under the cake and remove paper. Place on cooling rack.

When cold join the cakes together with Cream Cheese Filling.

To Prepare Topping: Mix all ingredients together until well combined.

To Prepare Cream Cheese Filling: Mix all ingredients until smooth.

SUFFICIENT FOR TWO 18 CM (7 IN) SANDWICH CAKE TINS

ZUCCHINI (COURGETTE) APPLE AND WALNUT CAKE

1½ cups (375 ml/12 fl oz) light oil

2 cups (500 g/16 oz) raw sugar

4 eggs

1 zucchini (courgette) 125 g (4 oz), trimmed and grated

1 green skinned apple, peeled, cored and grated

75 g (2½ oz) walnuts, chopped

125 g (4 oz) self-raising flour

125 g (4 oz) plain flour

1 teaspoon bicarbonate of soda

1 teaspoon ground cinnamon

Note: This recipe can be halved to make one cake. Otherwise make the full recipe and freeze one half (cooked or uncooked) until required.

Preheat oven to 150°C (300°F).

Beat oil and sugar together for 5 minutes. Beat eggs in, one at a time. Add zucchini (courgette), apple and walnuts. Sift flours, bicarbonate of soda and cinnamon together and fold into mixture. Spoon into two greased and lined 18 cm (7 in)

sandwich tins. Bake for 1 hour. Test with a fine skewer. Turn out to cool.

When cool ice with chocolate icing (see recipe page 74).

SUFFICIENT FOR TWO 18 CM (7 IN) SANDWICH CAKE TINS

ICED PUMPKIN CAKE

250 g (8 oz) sugar

185 g (6 oz) unsalted butter

½ teaspoon vanilla essence

2 eggs

185 g (6 oz) dried fruit, chopped

1 cup cooked mashed pumpkin

125 g (4 oz) self-raising flour

125 g (4 oz) plain flour

1 teaspoon bicarbonate of soda

½ cup (125 ml/4 fl oz) milk

Preheat oven to 150°C (300°F).

Cream sugar and butter together until white and fluffy. Add vanilla and beat in eggs, one at a time. Add dried fruit and pumpkin, stir well. Sift flours and bicarbonate of soda together. Fold in half the flour with half the milk, stir until smooth. Add remaining flour and milk, stir well.

Spoon into greased and lined 23 cm (9 in) springform cake tin. Bake for 1 hour or until cooked. Turn out onto a wire cooling rack, remove greaseproof paper. Cool well before icing. See cake toppings and icings, page 74.

Variations: Substitute one of the following for dried fruit: 1 cup chopped dates; 1 cup chopped sultanas plus 1 tablespoon of orange juice; 1 cup currants plus 1 teaspoon of mixed spice.

CARROT AND ZUCCHINI (COURGETTE) GATEAU

....

4 eggs

250 g (8 oz) sugar

¾ cup (185 ml/6 fl oz) oil

125 g (4 oz) self-raising flour

125 g (4 oz) plain flour

1 teaspoon bicarbonate of soda

1 teaspoon ground cinnamon

1 carrot, scraped and grated

1 zucchini (courgette) trimmed, grated (approximately 125 g/4 oz)

125 g (4 oz) ground hazelnuts

Note: This recipe can be halved to make one cake. Otherwise make the full recipe and freeze one half (cooked or uncooked) until required.

Preheat oven to 150°C (300°F).

Beat eggs, sugar and oil together until white. Sift flours, bicarbonate of soda and cinnamon together, fold into mixture. Stir in vegetables and hazelnuts. Spoon into two greased and lined 18 cm (7 in) sandwich cake tins.

Bake for 40 minutes to 1 hour. Test with a fine skewer. Cool. Cut each cake in half through the middle. Join each of the layers together with cheese icing (see recipe page 74) and top with more cheese icing.

SUFFICIENT FOR TWO 18 CM (7 IN) SANDWICH CAKE TINS

HARVEST CAKE

....

1½ cups (375 ml/12 fl oz) light oil

375 g (12 oz) sugar

3 eggs

Carrot And Zucchini (Courgette) Gateau (recipe below) and Steamed Pumpkin Pudding with Apple Caramel (page 71)

1 cup cooked mashed pumpkin

185 g (6 oz) brown rice flour

125 g (4 oz) gluten free flour

1 teaspoon bicarbonate of soda

1 teaspoon ground cinnamon

½ teaspoon ground nutmeg

¼ teaspoon ground cloves

125 g (4 oz) chopped walnuts

TOPPING

1 tablespoon washed pumpkin seeds and/or 1 tablespoon sugar mixed with half a tablespoon of ground cinnamon

Note: This cake is a gluten free cake.

Preheat oven to 150°C (300°F).

Beat oil and sugar together until creamy. Beat in eggs one at a time.

Add pumpkin. Sift flours (reserving the husks), bicarbonate of soda and spices. Return husks to flour. Stir flour into mixture, add walnuts and mix.

Spoon into a greased and lined 18 cm (7 in) cake tin. Bake for 45 minutes. Sprinkle with desired topping. Bake for a further 15 minutes. Test with a fine skewer.

Variation: Substitute rice flour for gluten free flour and/or add two, peeled, cored, sliced green apples, with or instead of walnuts.

Zucchini (Courgette) Wholemeal Pancake Stack (recipe above), Pumpkin Pancakes (page 78)

ZUCCHINI (COURGETTE) WHOLEMEAL PANCAKE STACK

....

1 egg

1 cup (250 ml/8 fl oz) milk

1 cup grated zucchini (courgette)

155 g (5 oz) wholemeal self-raising flour

oil for frying

Lightly beat egg and milk. Fold in zucchini (courgette) and sifted flour. Stand for 30 minutes at room temperature (if, after standing, the mixture is a little thick add more milk to make into a pouring consistency). Pour a little oil in a heavy based frying pan to grease it. Spoon in 1 tablespoon mixture, swirl to spread. Allow to bubble, then turn with a palette knife or egg slice. Cook other side. Keep warm, by covering with a clean tea towel which has been wrung out in warm water. Repeat until all mixture is used.

To Serve: Spread each layer with filling of your choice, place one on top of the other to make a stack.

Note: Pancakes will freeze well for months, wrapped separately between layers of plastic wrap.

MAKES 12

PUMPKIN PANCAKES

1 egg

125 g (4 oz) plain flour

1 cup cooked, mashed pumpkin

beer, to mix

oil, for frying

Mix egg, sifted flour and pumpkin together. Beat in sufficient beer to make a thick, pouring consistency. Pour a little oil into a heavy based frying pan and heat. Pour in 1 tablespoon of mixture, swirl to spread. Allow to bubble. Turn with a palette knife or egg slice, cook other side. Keep warm in a clean moist tea towel previously wrung out in warm water. Repeat, using all the mixture.

To Serve: Fill centre of pancake with desired filling, roll up. Serve with salad and brown rice.

Pancakes will freeze well for months, wrapped separately between layers of plastic wrap.

MAKES 12

SAVOURY FILLINGS FOR PUMPKIN PANCAKES

TUNA CREAM

1 small can tuna, drained

125 g (4 oz) thick sour cream

1 tablespoon finely chopped onion

1 tablespoon chopped fresh parsley

Combine all ingredients.

Variation: Substitute, cooked, diced chicken for tuna.

CHEESY FILLING

125 g (4 oz) cottage cheese

4 fresh basil leaves, chopped

pinch of dried thyme

Combine all ingredients.

CHICKEN LIVER FILLING

60 g (2 oz) butter

250 g (8 oz) chicken livers, washed and sliced

2 shallots (spring onions) sliced

6 mushrooms, finely sliced

2 sprigs parsley, chopped

squeeze of lemon juice

freshly ground black pepper

30 g (1 oz) butter, extra

1 tablespoon plain flour

pinch salt

½ cup (125 ml/4 fl oz) water

1 chicken stock cube

½ cup (125 g/4 fl oz) cream

125 g (4 oz) Gruyere cheese, grated

To Prepare Filling: Heat butter in a frying pan and fry chicken livers, stirring until livers are just cooked (approximately 5 minutes). Add mushrooms and shallots, cook a further 2 minutes, stirring all the time. Stir in parsley, lemon juice and a dash of pepper. Remove from heat.

To Prepare in Microwave: Cook livers in butter on HIGH for 3 minutes, add remaining ingredients stir. Cook for a further 2 minutes on HIGH.

To Prepare Sauce: Heat extra butter in a saucepan, stir in flour and salt. Remove from heat, add water, stock cube and cream, mix well. Return to heat, stir until sauce thickens.

To Prepare in Microwave: Melt butter on HIGH for 30 seconds. Stir in other ingredients, cook on HIGH for 2 minutes, stir well. Cook a further 1 minute on HIGH or until sauce is thick. Beat well.

To Serve: Fill pancakes, coat with sauce, sprinkle cheese on top, grill or bake until cheese just starts to bubble.

SWEET FILLINGS FOR PUMPKIN PANCAKES

To make sweet pumpkin pancakes, follow the recipe for pumpkin pancakes and add 1 tablespoon of icing sugar and 1 teaspoon of ground cinnamon to the sifted flour.

APPLE

2 green skinned apples peeled, sliced

1 teaspoon ground cinnamon

1 tablespoon icing sugar

1 tablespoon brandy or Grand Marnier (optional)

Cook the apples in a small amount of water in a saucepan until soft. Mix in the cinnamon, sugar and brandy or liqueur. Spoon apple mixture in centre of a pancake. Roll up and top with whipped cream.

Variation: Add 1 tablespoon sultanas to apples.

ALMOND

125 g (4 oz) ground or crushed almonds

20 g (½ oz) butter, melted

2 tablespoons honey

Combine all ingredients. Place warm pancake on a dessert plate, spoon filling into centre. Roll up. Serve with a scoop of ice cream.

Bread has formed a staple part of European diet for centuries, with each country developing a bread to suit its own particular cuisine.

PUMPKIN LOAF

This is a heavy textured bread and is absolutely delicious eaten freshly cooked.

95 g (3 oz) plain flour

½ teaspoon baking powder

½ teaspoon each, ground nutmeg, cloves and cinnamon

60 g (2 oz) sugar

30 g (1 oz) chopped walnuts

2 tablespoons chopped dates

¼ cup (60 ml/2 fl oz) oil

1 tablespoon water

1 egg, beaten

1 cup cooked mashed pumpkin

Preheat oven to 180°C (350°F).

Sift flour and baking powder together in a mixing bowl. Add all remaining ingredients and mix well. Spoon into a greased loaf tin. Bake for 1 hour. Cool in tin.

To Serve: Slice whilst warm and spread with butter.

PUMPKIN MUFFINS

1 cup (250 ml/8 fl oz) milk

squeeze of lemon juice

60 g (2 oz) sugar

60 g (2 oz) butter

1 egg, beaten

210 g (7 oz) self-raising flour

pinch salt

1 cup cooked, mashed pumpkin

Preheat oven to 190°C (375°F).

Combine milk and lemon juice (this will sour the milk, making it lighter). Beat sugar and butter together until creamy. Add egg. Sift flour and salt, fold in alternately with milk. Mix in pumpkin. Spoon mixture into 12 greased muffin pans. Bake for 20 minutes. Turn out and serve whilst hot with butter.

Variation: Substitute 1 grated zucchini (courgette) or 1 cup of cooked and mashed marrow for pumpkin.

MAKES 12 MUFFINS

Muffins and scones originate from the hearth or flat baking stones of ancient times. The Scottish poet, Robert Burns wrote of bannocks o' barley, also known in America as cupcakes.

Perfect for freezing, either cooked or uncooked. Cook while still frozen.

SAVOURY ZUCCHINI (COURGETTE) SCONES

250 g (8 oz) self-raising flour

pinch salt

30 g (1 oz) butter

1 zucchini (courgette) (approximately 125 g/4 oz), cooked and mashed

1 egg, beaten

½ cup (125 ml/4 fl oz) cold milk

1 tablespoon grated cheese

pinch of dried thyme

cold water, to mix

extra milk, for glazing

Preheat oven to 225°C (425°F).

Sift flour and salt into a bowl. With fingertips, rub in butter, then cut in zucchini (courgette) with a knife. Cut in egg, milk, cheese and thyme. Mixture should have formed a firm dough. If not binding together, add a little cold water. Sprinkle a sheet of greaseproof paper with extra flour, turn out dough. Knead lightly to form a smooth ball. Pat out to a 2 cm (¾ in) thickness, cut with a 5 cm (2 in) scone cutter. Place on greased baking tray, brush with a little extra milk. Bake 10 minutes or until brown.

Serve hot with butter.

MAKES 12

SWEET PUMPKIN SCONES

310 g (10 oz) self raising flour

pinch salt

1 teaspoon mixed spice

40 g (1½ oz) butter

½ cup cooked pumpkin, mashed

1 egg beaten

cold milk

Preheat oven to 225°C (425°F).

Sift flour, salt and spice into a bowl. Rub in butter with fingertips until it has a sandly texture. Stir in pumpkin, egg and sufficient milk to make into a soft dough.

Sprinkle a piece of greaseproof paper with extra flour. Turn out dough, knead lightly until a smooth ball forms. Pat dough out to approximately 2 cm (¾ in) thickness. Cut dough with a scone cutter dipped in flour. Place scones on a greased oven tray. Brush tops with a little milk. Bake for 10 minutes or until brown on top.

Serve with lots of butter or jam and cream.

Variations: Add 1 tablespoon of sultanas and 1 tablespoon honey and mix in with the egg, or add 1 tablespoon chopped walnuts and a pinch of ginger with the flour.

MAKES 12

AUSSIE DAMPER

In outback Australia, the damper was prepared by winding the dough around a stick, then cooked over an open fire, dipped in golden syrup and eaten, hot.

ZUCCHINI (COURGETTE) DAMPER

This damper does not keep well, best eaten immediately.

375 g (12 oz) self-raising flour

pinch salt

60 g (2 oz) butter

½ cup (125 ml/4 fl oz) milk

½ cup (125 ml/4 fl oz) water

1 zucchini (courgette) trimmed, cooked, mashed (approximately 100 g/3½ oz)

extra flour, for sprinkling

extra milk for, glazing

Preheat oven to 200°C (400°F).

Sift flour and salt into a bowl. With fingertips, rub in butter. Cut in milk and water with a knife. Add zucchini (courgette). Turn dough out onto a lightly floured board or sheet of greaseproof paper. Knead lightly just until dough forms a smooth ball. Pat into a 15 cm (6 in) circle. Place on a greased baking tray. With a knife cut a cross 1 cm (½ in) deep. Brush top with a little milk, dust with extra flour. Bake for 10 minutes then reduce heat to 180°C (350°F) and cook a further 15 minutes.

Serve immediately, with lots of butter.

SWEET PUMPKIN MOUSSE

1 packet green or yellow jelly crystals

300 ml (10 fl oz) cream

2 eggs, separated

1 cup cooked pumpkin, mashed

85 g (3 oz) brown sugar

1 teaspoon ground cinnamon

extra whipped cream and a teaspoon of ground ginger, to decorate

Make up jelly according to directions on packet. Rinse 6 parfait glasses or glass bowls with cold water, drain, but do not dry. Half fill glasses with jelly. Chill until set.

Whip cream until thick. Whisk egg whites until stiff. Combine egg yolks, pumpkin, sugar, and cinnamon. Fold in cream then fold in egg whites. Spoon on top of set jelly. Chill thoroughly.

To serve: Whip cream with ginger until thick and pile on top of mousse.

SERVES 6

MOUSSE

Mousse is French for 'mossy'. A light, frothy and chilled sweet made with egg whites and cream.

Pictured on previous pages: Sweet Pumpkin Scones, Zucchini (Courgette) Damper (recipes above)

Ice Cream

*T*he delights of ice cream, have been known for many centuries. The Chinese introduced the art to the Indians who in turn passed it on to the Persians and Arabs. Europe was not included until the middle of the 15th century. The first colonists to North America took the recipe with them and the first commercial factory was established in Baltimore in 1851.

SPICY ICE CREAM

Preparation for this recipe starts the day before the dish is needed. This ice cream does not require double freezing.

> 1 (375 ml/12 fl oz) can evaporated milk
>
> 1 tablespoon gelatine
>
> 1 tablespoon hot water
>
> ½ cup cooked and mashed pumpkin
>
> 60 g (2 oz) brown sugar
>
> ½ teaspoon ground nutmeg
>
> ½ teaspoon ground cinnamon

Place unopened can of evaporated milk in a pan and half fill the pan with water. Bring to boil, simmer for 10 minutes. Remove from pan, cool can thoroughly. Place in refrigerator, chill overnight.

Pour evaporated milk into a bowl and beat for 2 minutes with an electric mixer. Dissolve gelatine in hot water, add along with all other ingredients and beat for a further 1 minute. Pour into a 2 litre (64 fl oz) freezer-proof container. Place in the freezer until firm.

MAKES 2 LITRES (64 FL OZ)

RICH WALNUT ICE CREAM

> 3 eggs
>
> 45 g (1½ oz) brown sugar
>
> 1 tablespoon honey
>
> ½ cup pumpkin, cooked and mashed
>
> 300 ml (10 fl oz) thick cream
>
> 60 g (2 oz) walnuts, crushed

In a saucepan, beat eggs, sugar and honey together. Stir over heat until mixture starts to simmer (or microwave on LOW for 2 minutes). Remove from heat, stir well.

Cool slightly then beat in pumpkin until smooth. Stir in cream. Place in ice cream maker for 35 minutes. Add walnuts and beat for a further 5 minutes. Freeze.

If you don't have an ice cream maker, place the mixture in a shallow freezer-proof container, freeze until mixture starts to thicken around edges. Spoon into a bowl and beat with an electric beater until thick and creamy. Re-freeze until firm.

Note: Ice cream makers vary, so follow manufacturer's directions.

SERVES 6 TO 8

Preserves and Craft

*M*aking your own jams, pickles or chutneys is a satisfying, creative experience. Top the jars with a circle of material and secure with a ribbon. Friends will be delighted with your handmade gift.

PUMPKIN JAM (JELLY)

This jam has a lovely golden colour, is easy to cook, and has a great taste.

- 1.5 kg (3 lb) pumpkin, peel, remove seeds, dice
- 300 ml (10 fl oz) lemon juice
- 1 kg (2 lb) sugar
- 2 tablespoons fresh ginger, finely chopped, discard fibres
- 5 cups (1.25 litres/40 fl oz) water

Place pumpkin, lemon juice and sugar in a deep pan. Add ginger and water. Stir over heat until sugar dissolves. Bring to the boil. Boil uncovered without stirring for 1½ hours (this jam is a little prone to catch on the bottom of the pan so watch carefully). Mash or purée the jam if you desire a smoother consistency.

Pour into heated jars. Allow to cool thoroughly before sealing.

Variation: Add the pulp of 4 passionfruit with other ingredients, or add 90 g (3 oz) dried, chopped apricots with other ingredients.

MAKES APPROXIMATELY 6 CUPS

PRESERVING

Preserving is a form of cooking which prevents foods from decaying, making them suitable for future use.

PUMPKIN CUCUMBER MARMALADE

- 4 large oranges
- 1 lemon, medium size
- 500 g (16 oz) pumpkin, peeled and diced.
- 1 medium cucumber, peeled, seeded, diced
- 12 cups (3 litres/96 fl oz) water
- 1.25 kg (40 oz) sugar

Peel oranges and lemon thinly without pith. Place rind in a bowl. Pull away remaining pith from flesh, remove seeds and place pith and seeds in a cloth (a piece of muslin, fine cotton or a well washed foot of new pantyhose are all suitable) and tie securely. Break oranges and lemon into segments, place in a bowl with rind, add wrapped pith and seeds. Cover with warm water and stand overnight. Next day, remove cloth with pith and seeds and discard. Drain fruit, discarding water.

Place diced pumpkin, cucumber, fruit and 3 litres (96 fl oz) water in a deep pan. Cover. Bring to boil, simmer for 2 hours. Stir in sugar, stirring until dissolved, allow to boil rapidly without stirring for 20 minutes. Pour into warmed jars. Cool before sealing.

Variation: 2 green skinned apples, peeled, seeded in place of cucumber.

MAKES APPROXIMATELY 6 CUPS

RELISHES

Relishes are sharp, tangy, pulpy vegetables or fruit, containing sugar and vinegar. Once opened they should be refrigerated. Serve with hot or cold meats.

Pictured on previous pages: Zucchini (Courgette) Relish, Pumpkin Jam (Jelly) and Choko Chutney (recipes these pages)

ZUCCHINI (COURGETTE) RELISH

750 g (24 oz) zucchini (courgette) (approximately 5 to 6) trimmed

1 tablespoon salt

3 large tomatoes, peeled

500 g (16 oz) onions, peeled

125 g (4 oz) raisins

2 cups (500 ml/16 fl oz) brown vinegar

¼ cup (60 ml/2 fl oz) water

500 g (16 oz) brown sugar

1 teaspoon garam masala

Place washed zucchini (courgette) in a colander, sprinkle with salt and stand for 2 hours. Rinse in cold water, drain. Chop tomatoes, zucchini (courgette), and onions, place in a deep pan with raisins, vinegar and water. Cover and bring to the boil. Simmer for 30 minutes. Stir in sugar, and garam masala, stir until sugar dissolves, allow to boil. Simmer for a further 20 minutes or until thick. Pour into warmed jars. Allow to cool overnight. Seal.

Variation: Add 3 green skinned apples, peeled, sliced and cooked with vegetables.

MAKES APPROXIMATELY 4 CUPS

CHOKO OR CUCUMBER PICKLES

750 g (24 oz) chokos or cucumbers, peeled, seeded and diced

2 onions, sliced

1 tablespoon salt

4 cups (1 litre/32 fl oz) white vinegar

60 g (2 oz) sugar

10 cloves

1 teaspoon ground ginger

½ teaspoon allspice

DRESSING

1 tablespoon cornflour

1 teaspoon ground turmeric

2 tablespoons dry mustard

extra 2 cups (500 ml/16 fl oz) vinegar

250 g (8 oz) sugar

Sprinkle vegetables with salt, stand overnight. Drain and rinse, place in a deep pan with vinegar, sugar and spices, stir over heat until sugar dissolves, Bring to the boil, simmer without stirring for 20 minutes or until liquid has almost evaporated.

To Prepare Dressing: Mix cornflour with turmeric, mustard and extra vinegar, stir into vegetables. Add sugar, stir over heat until sugar dissolves. Bring to the boil, simmer for 5 minutes. Remove and discard the 10 cloves. Spoon into jars. Seal only when cold.

MAKES APPROXIMATELY 4 CUPS

CHOKO CHUTNEY

Gramma or pumpkin may be substituted for choko in this recipe.

1.5 kg (3 lb) chokos, peeled, seed removed and diced

2 green skinned apples, peeled, cored and chopped

1 onion, diced

375 g (12 oz) sultanas

½ teaspoon ground cardamom

1 teaspoon ground cinnamon

2 cups (500 ml/16 fl oz) brown vinegar

1 cup (250 ml/8 fl oz) water

· 250 g (8 oz) brown sugar

pinch chilli powder

2 bananas, peeled and sliced

Combine all ingredients except bananas in a deep pan. Stir until sugar has dissolved. Bring to the boil, simmer without stirring for 1½ hours. Add bananas, continue to simmer for a further 10 minutes or until thick. Pour into heated jars. Seal when cold.

MAKES APPROXIMATELY 6 CUPS

ZUCCHINI (COURGETTE) CHUTNEY

- 750 g (24 oz) zucchini (courgette) trimmed
- 1 tablespoon salt
- 250 g (8 oz) tomatoes, peeled and chopped
- 125 g (4 oz) onions, peeled and chopped
- 90 g (3 oz) sultanas
- 500 g (16 oz) sugar
- 1½ cups (375 ml/12 fl oz) white vinegar
- 1 teaspoon mixed spice

Sprinkle zucchini (courgette) with salt and stand for 1 hour. Rinse and drain. Place in a deep pan with all ingredients, stir over heat until sugar dissolves. Bring to the boil. Simmer until thick. Spoon into warmed jars. Seal only when cold.

Variation: Before bottling, add 125 g (8 oz) chopped walnuts.

MAKES APPROXIMATELY 6 CUPS

PICKLES

Pickles fall into two categories, clear with spicy vinegar, or thick and pulpy. Serve with cold meats. Refrigerate once opened.

CUCUMBER RELISH

- 2 medium cucumbers, chopped
- 4 red capsicums (peppers) seeded and sliced
- 4 green capsicums (peppers) seeded and sliced
- 3 tomatoes peeled and chopped
- 3 onions, sliced
- 1½ cups (375 ml/12 fl oz) water
- 1½ cups (375 ml/12 fl oz) white vinegar
- 375 g (12 oz) sugar
- 1 teaspoon mixed spice
- 1 tablespoon cornflour
- 2 tablespoons extra water
- 2 teaspoons mustard seeds (or seeded mustard)

Combine all vegetables in a deep pan, stir in water, vinegar, sugar and spice and stir over heat until sugar dissolves. Bring to the boil, simmer for 1½ hours or until mixture is thick. Blend cornflour with extra water, add mustard seeds or mustard and stir into relish. Bring back to boil stirring continuously. Spoon into warm jars. Seal when completely cold.

MAKES APPROXIMATELY 6 TO 7 CUPS

CHUTNEY

Originally of Indian origin, chutney is served as a side dish to curries. Once opened, it should be refrigerated.

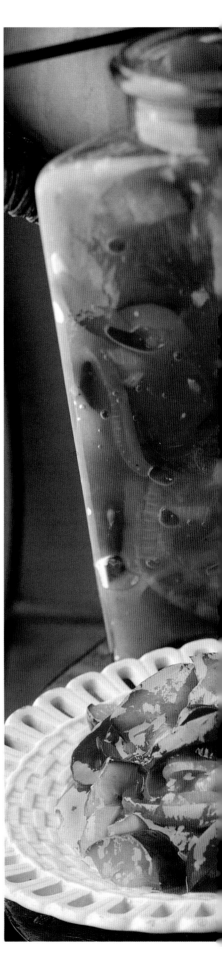

Cucumber Relish (recipe above), Pumpkin Cucumber Marmalade (page 86)

Traditional Hallowe'en Containers

*T*he word "Hallowe'en" immediately brings to mind pumpkin lanterns. Hallowe'en (shortened from All-hallow-even) celebrations precede All Saints' Day. It originated in Druid times when the people were afraid that as winter approached, the long nights would be haunted by ghosts and witches, so they lit bonfires and made sacrifices to pacify the evil spirits.

With the advent of Christianity, this custom changed to a festival of fun where children wore scary masks and went around on Hallowe'en asking for alms. When the gifts were received the recipient prayed for the lost souls who may have been tempted to haunt the house.

Little has changed, children still dress up in scary costumes and 'trick 'n treat' receiving sweets in payment for not playing pranks. Bonfires are still lit and pumpkins become grinning candle holders, also used to frighten away the evil spirits.

JACK O' LANTERN

1 large pumpkin
3 candles
aluminium foil
straight pins

Choose a large pumpkin. On the top of the pumpkin, draw a circle to form a lid. With a sharp knife, cut around the circle and lift the lid out.

Remove seeds and membrane from centre of the pumpkin, scrape out the flesh leaving a 3 cm (1½ in) thick wall.

With a pencil, trace a face on the side of the pumpkin shell. Using a skewer, poke a few holes into the drawing so that you can insert a knife to cut out the features.

Place the candles in crunched foil and secure foil to pumpkin base with straight pins.

Light candles and replace lid, allow candles to burn a few minutes.

Remove the lid, there will be a 'smoke' circle on the inside of the lid. Carefully cut this small circle out to form a 'chimney'. Replace the lid.

Note: If a piece is cut, or broken in error, re-attach with a toothpick.

PUMPKIN POTS

small golden nugget pumpkins
oil

Cut tops from vegetables.

Scoop out seeds and membrane, leaving a thickish wall.

Scrape flesh from tops and, with a pencil, mark a half circle on edge to form a space for a small spoon handle to protrude. Cut the spoon hole.

Brush outside with oil to give a shiny appearance.

Use as pots for holding condiments (mustards, sauces, mayonnaise etc) for buffets or barbecues.

SMALL CANDLE HOLDERS

These look great as candle holders on a barbecue table.

small pumpkins or squash
small candles
foil
straight pins

Follow directions for pots, except on the lid you will need to make a chimney hole (follow chimney directions in "Jack O' Lantern") instead of a spoon hole.

With a pencil, mark little windows around shell, pierce with a skewer and insert knife to cut out the windows.

Wrap the base of a small candle with crunched foil and secure foil based candle to base of shell with straight pins.

Creative Garnishes

CUCUMBER SLICES

With a vegetable peeler, cut strips of skin 0.5 cm (¼ in) apart the full length of the cucumber. Discard strips.

Cut cucumber into round slices.

Use in salads.

CUCUMBER CONES

With the skin on, thinly slice cucumber into rounds.

Cut from centre of round to the edge.

Hold each side, twist to form a cone.

Use as a garnish for savouries, or fill with a little pâté.

CUCUMBER SPIRALS

With a vegetable peeler, peel skin in a continuous spiral.

Wind spiral tightly.

Use as a garnish for drinks.

CUCUMBER BUTTERFLY

Cut cucumber into thin round slices.

Cut each slice in half.

Keeping the centre of the half circle joined, cut through to outer edge then turn to form butterfly wings.

Use as a garnish for savouries.

CUCUMBER LEAF

Lengthwise, thickly cut cucumber into slices. Then cut slices into rectangles, approximately 6 cm x 3 cm (2½ in x 1 in).

Cut a leaf shape from each piece.

Score a centre vein, and light marks to form side veins.

Place in ice water and allow to curl slightly.

Use as a garnish for savouries.

ZUCCHINI (COURGETTE) STRIPS

With a vegetable peeler, thinly slice zucchini (courgette) lengthwise.

Use as a garnish for salads.

Pictured on following pages:
Jack O' Lantern, Pumpkin Pots

"Pumpkins in fairy tales, pumpkins in rhymes,
Pumpkins endure throughout the times.
For puddings and custards, soups and for pies,
Our pumpkins and squashes are common supplies.
Humble yet handy, a fodder, a treat,
If it were not for pumpkin, life's not complete."

Measuring Made Easy

How to Measure Liquids

METRIC	IMPERIAL	CUPS
30 ml	1 fl oz	1 tablespoon plus 2 teaspoons
60 ml	2 fl oz	¼ cup
90 ml	3 fl oz	
125 ml	4 fl oz	½ cup
150 ml	5 fl oz	
170 ml	5½ fl oz	
180 ml	6 fl oz	¾ cup
220 ml	7 fl oz	
250 ml	8 fl oz	1 cup
500 ml	16 fl oz	2 cups
600 ml	20 fl oz (1 pint)	2½ cups

How to Measure Dry Ingredients

15 g	½ oz	
30 g	1 oz	
60 g	2 oz	
90 g	3 oz	
125 g	4 oz	(¼ lb)
155 g	5 oz	
185 g	6 oz	
220 g	7 oz	
250 g	8 oz	(½ lb)
280 g	9 oz	
315 g	10 oz	
345 g	11 oz	
375 g	12 oz	(¾ lb)
410 g	13 oz	
440 g	14 oz	
470 g	15 oz	
500 g	16 oz	(1 lb)
750 g	24 oz	(1½ lb)
1 kg	32 oz	(2 lb)

Quick Conversions

5 mm	¼ in	
1 cm	½ in	
2 cm	¾ in	
2.5 cm	1 in	
5 cm	2 in	
6 cm	2½ in	
8 cm	3 in	
10 cm	4 in	
12 cm	5 in	
15 cm	6 in	
18 cm	7 in	
20 cm	8 in	
23 cm	9 in	
25 cm	10 in	
28 cm	11 in	
30 cm	12 in	(1 ft)
46 cm	18 in	
50 cm	20 in	
61 cm	24 in	(2 ft)

Note:

We developed the recipes in this book in Australia where the tablespoon measure is 20 ml. In many other countries the tablespoon is 15 ml. For most recipes this difference will not be noticeable. However, for recipes using baking powder, gelatine, bicarbonate of soda, small amounts of flour and cornflour, we suggest you add an extra teaspoon for each tablespoon specified.

Using Cups and Spoons

All cup and spoon measurements are level

METRIC CUP

¼ cup	60 ml	2 fl oz
⅓ cup	80 ml	2½ fl oz
½ cup	125 ml	4 fl oz
1 cup	250 ml	8 fl oz

METRIC SPOONS

¼ teaspoon	1.25 ml
½ teaspoon	2.5 ml
1 teaspoon	5 ml
1 tablespoon	20 ml

Oven Temperatures

TEMPERATURES	CELSIUS (°C)	FAHRENHEIT (°F)	GAS MARK
Very slow	120	250	½
Slow	150	300	2
Moderately slow	160-180	325-350	3-4
Moderate	190-200	375-400	5-6
Moderately hot	220-230	425-450	7
Hot	250-260	475-500	8-9

Index